DRAFT-DODGING ODYSSEY

By

Ken Kiask

ISBN: 1508751692
ISBN-13: 978-1508751694

PREFACE

This is a true story. Aside from some embellishments here and there and a made-up incident or two (incidental to the story), this is the way it happened. For making it happen, I thank the foreign policy mavens who got us into an unending war in Vietnam which split a generation; the people of the Third World, who treated me with courtesy and kindness, passion and compassion; and Samira, for being who she is.

KEN KIASK

CHAPTERS

CHAPTER 1 - DEPARTURE

"Viet what?" I replied abstractedly to the coed's earnest query "What do you think about Vietnam?" I was being facetious, of course. It was 1967 and everyone my age, especially those who, like me, faced the possibility of being drafted into the army, had an opinion on Vietnam. But, in reality, my response wasn't totally off the mark. I'd never been politically oriented and the all-consuming conflict in Southeast Asia, then at its height, had entered my consciousness but not particularly piqued my interest.

This despite a brush with political activism a year earlier. While attending the Stanford Business School, I had met David Harris, president of the student body and an early draft resister. Harris gained local fame when some fraternity boys grabbed him one night and shaved off his unseemly (from their point of view) long locks (Long hair was symbolic back then - until construction workers adopted the style). Two years later Harris gained national prominence and became the face of resistance to the draft when he married folksinger Joan Baez.

I was at a dorm party on the campus of the University of Texas, heading south with Bill and his wife, Kathy, on a trip which, as planned, would take us down the Pan American Highway all the way to Chile and then across the continent to Rio de Janeiro just in time for Carnival. I had dropped out of the business school after completing the first year of the two-year MBA program. Now I felt like doing a little traveling before settling down to post-college life.

Problem was Uncle Sam had different plans for me. Not being enrolled in college anymore meant I would lose my 2-S Selective Service deferment as a student and be reclassified 1-A, and 1-A's were being invited to try on a pair of khakis pretty quickly at that time. I had neglected to inform my draft board I was no longer in school (inadvertently, of course), so I still had my 2-S. But it was November now and I suspected the board would figure it out for themselves soon enough when they didn't receive the required Proof of Enrollment for the current academic year. I had also neglected to inform them I was leaving the country, as the law required.

"Fulfilling your military obligation", as it was put to us in those days - in tones suggesting it was as inevitable as death and taxes - vexed a generation's life plans. When asked by the committee interviewing me for a Fulbright scholarship my senior year at Dartmouth "And how, Mr. Kiask, do you plan on fulfilling your military obligation?", I had responded "I don't, if I can help it," mindlessly forgetting who it was that funded the Fulbright program (the US government), but I think aptly capsulizing the attitude of most of my peers towards the draft. (I didn't get the Fulbright.)

It wasn't that we were unpatriotic, at least I don't think so. If there had been a real national emergency, we would have answered the call dutifully, perhaps even enthusiastically, as our fathers had in their time. We just didn't see home and hearth being threatened by some small, impoverished nation in far-off, Southeast Asia. As for more potent foes, the Cold War, which had inspired our permanent state of military preparedness, promised such instantaneous, total annihilation that by the time the need for a supply of pimply-faced, innocent-as-lambs, cannon fodder materialized, the source of supply would have been vaporized.

"Evading The Draft" was a parlor game all of us draft-age men played. We ruminated on off-the-wall strategies for avoiding military service, from knocking a girl up and marrying her to take advantage of the exemption for fathers to trading our citizenship for that of Costa Rica, a country which has no army. Some popular strategies actually pursued included slipping across the border into Canada, burning your draft card and going to prison, and, ironically, enlisting, to get a better deal. You won the game if you successfully evaded the draft. If you lost, you went to Vietnam. Capturing a much-coveted spot in the National Guard got you a draw.

I had participated in the game along with everyone else, but hadn't really given "fulfilling my military obligation" much serious thought. As long as I had my 2-S, the draft was too remote a contingency to plan for, and I still had my 2-S. The cynical observer might conclude from my leaving the country that I was not planning to serve. But I don't think that was true. That would imply I had a plan and, as far as I can recollect, I didn't. I've never been very good at planning ahead, and my plans then didn't go beyond a cross-continental jaunt capped with lolling on some tropical beach. I knew the draft issue would come up, but I hoped I had a couple of months before I was reclassified and received my notice to report for duty. Until then, I looked forward to seeing a little of Latin America.

The trip hadn't even been my idea. Bill, scion of a wealthy Dallas family, had come up with it. For some reason, he invited me to come along. My relationship with Bill had always been ambiguous. It went back a long way, all the way to grade school. It was grounded in friendship, but there was always the underlying disparity in our socioeconomic status, which resulted in certain disparities in our contributions to the friendship. As a rule, Bill provided the means and I provided the manpower, meaning while I enjoyed the privilege of riding his horses or vacationing at this family's beach house, it was understood that, if there was any dirty work to be done, I would be the one to do it. I like to think I put up with this not because of any admiration of or craving for wealth, but simply because I was a pushover. This was true vis-à-vis everyone, not just Bill. It's just that Bill took advantage of my weakness more often than others did. Now Bill was providing the car and the gas, and I was there, in part no doubt for companionship, but perhaps more importantly as the handyman, go-for, and donkey. If we suffered a flat tire, there was no question who would be the one to change it.

As we approached the border, I was a bit apprehensive. I had visions of some burly border guard dragging me out of the car, sneering, "Boy, you ain't agoin' nowheres. Your draft board warned us ya might try an' run for it. Get in that van! It's takin' ya back to Dallas." But no such thing happened. We were waved through without so much as having to show our passports. I breathed easier once on the Mexican side of the Rio Grande.

Chapter 2 – ACAPULCO

Bill, his wife Kathy, and I traveled south through Mexico compatibly enough, which was something of a surprise to me as my traveling companions were almost newlyweds, having married just three months previous. I couldn't help feeling like the third who makes a crowd, but they didn't seem to mind.

In the evening, after a day on the road, we would pull up to the swankiest hotel in whatever town we happened to be and Bill and Kathy would check in, while I spread out my sleeping bag in the back of the station wagon. While they dined at the poshest restaurant in town, I would partake of the fare at some more proletarian eatery. I had no complaints. I was having a great time and didn't really envy them their lifestyle. I felt I was gaining more authentic insights into Mexican culture down at my level.

Everything went fine until we got to Acapulco. As per our usual routine, Bill and Kathy were ensconced in some opulent beach-side hotel, and I was sleeping in the back of the car. But, hey, the car was parked just a block off the beach; the facilities of the finest hotels were available to me when nature called; and, if I felt the need for a shower, I could always impose on my traveling companions.

I spent the day prowling the beach in search of that elusive prey: comely young maidens. The beach was full of them, but my inept hunting technique would have reduced me to starvation had I been stalking them for sustenance, not the less vital but nonetheless imperative craving which was my real motivation. I was a late bloomer sex-wise. I'd lost my virginity just the previous summer, appropriately enough in San Francisco during its "Summer of Love". I liked the taste of carnality I'd gotten, and now my insatiable, testosterone-rich hormones goaded me on in the hunt. No half-starved, Neolithic hunter was ever more intent on his prey.

After a day or two of minimal success, I lucked on to a vacationing New Yorker whom I immediately fell in love with. She was as cute and perky as Doris Day, my lifelong notion of the perfect wife and lover. The three-year age differential was something of a problem (she being that much older than me), but she seemed to enjoy my company enough and allowed me to hang out with her and her companion, a young lady of considerably less allure physically, while they sought out more mature, better-heeled, strangers in the night. I was encouraged when they invited me to accompany them to a ritzy bar perched high on a cliff overlooking the Bay of Acapulco, though I suspected their interest in my company was limited to my potential usefulness as a bodyguard.

My fantasy of things to come later that evening were dashed almost before we'd ordered our first drinks when Tarzan swaggered into the bar and engaged my true love and her friend in conversation. By "Tarzan" I don't just mean some big, brawny hunk; I mean the *real* Tarzan. They were filming the TV series just outside Acapulco at the time, and this was one of the places the "swinger" - literal as well as figurative - hung out after hours. Tarzan was accompanied by his manager, a short, non-descript hustler I quickly labeled "sleazy". In no time the two had convinced my friends to join them for dinner, an invitation they inadvertently neglected to extend to me. I was left to nurse the one drink I felt I could afford to treat myself to in heartbroken solitude.

I heard the rest of the night's story the next day. For some reason, my sweetheart ended up with the manager, while Tarzan had to settle for second best. I chuckled smugly as my love interest related how the manager's sentiments towards her had proven considerably less Platonic than my own, and her friend described how Tarzan had behaved as if she were an alligator he was scripted to wrestle. My hopes, so cruelly dashed the previous evening, were raised, but, alas, in a day my sweetheart was on the plane back to New York, and I was left with nothing but a name and address, fond memories, and hopes for a future rendezvous (never to be fulfilled).

As I resumed my hormone-impelled quest, I was latched onto by a ten-year-old Mexican street urchin named Jose. Jose probably took me for a rich gringo he could easily cajole a few pesos from, the only mis-estimate of a mark I ever saw him make. Despite Jose's disappointment at my niggardly attitude toward philanthropy, we soon became boon companions as we shared a common lifestyle. We both spent our days on the beach and we both had an overriding interest in the young ladies, me for reasons already stated, he because they proved to be more susceptible to his charms, and hence more generous, than the men. At night I would retire to my luggage-sized sleeping chamber, while Jose crawled under the nearest bush.

My "Would you mind watching my clothes while I take a dip" approach with the ladies was generally less successful than his heart-rending life story artfully told. I tried to fool myself into believing his better success was due to a tactical advantage in that his line was basically true and sincere, while mine was blatantly transparent and profoundly shallow. Moreover, I reasoned to myself, his objective - nothing more than a few pesos - required less of a commitment on the part of his auditor than mine. But deep down I realized he was just better at it. He was aided by the circumstance that he was a cute little guy, with neat, though uncombed, jet black hair atop a round face with handsome Aztecan features: a chiseled nose, well-proportioned purplish lips, dark, penetrating eyes, and the complexion all the sun-burnt bodies on the beach were striving for. His English was remarkably good, considering, I suspect, he'd never attended a day of school.

"*Venga, Señor Keen,*" Jose beckoned to me one day, "We get some food now." I didn't know what he had in mind but followed him obediently up the beach to the back of the Acapulco Hilton.

"See," he said, pointing toward the large plate glass windows on the ground floor of the hotel, "In there." Inside, a crowd of neatly attired gringos was milling about a conference room. At the end of the room was a massive, taste-tempting buffet.

"You go get food. Bring me some," Jose instructed.

"But I can't go in there!" I protested, "I don't belong to that group."

"You American. They think you belong," Jose countered.

His logic was impeccable and I'd come to trust Jose's instincts about such things; but I hesitated, not being accustomed to being a freeloader and still sensitive, at that time, to public opprobrium. Badgered by Jose and enticed by the prospect of a free meal, I finally accepted the scheme and entered the hotel with an unsure gait and a guilt-ridden expression. I was sure "This guy sleeps in a car" was written all over my face; but, plucking up my courage, I sauntered into the conference room as if I belonged. I made a beeline for the buffet and soon had a plate stacked full of goodies. I felt like all eyes were on me, but looking around I saw that no one was paying me the slightest attention. Feeling like I'd just pulled off a heist comparable to the Brink's bank robbery, I walked out of the hotel, back to a grinning Jose.

"See, it easy... for you," Jose mumbled as he stuffed a Danish into his mouth?

As we wolfed down the food, I reflected on what I'd learned. Looking unmistakably like an American, or at worst a European, I could expect to get away with things I might not get away with back home. I could expect deferential treatment from native hotel staff, no matter how outrageous or presumptuous my behavior. This lesson would stand me in good stead in the months and years to come. Looking down at Jose happily stuffing his meal into his mouth, I smiled paternally.

"This little Mexican ragamuffin is teaching me, the college educated gringo, how to survive," I mused. I snickered to myself at the irony. What an eye-opener it would be for the intimidated, servile hotel staff if they knew how humble and grateful I felt at the moment toward one of their own... and a pint-sized one at that!

I often wonder what became of Jose. Did he turn his innocent, adolescent pursuit of women benefactors into a more calculated, manly livelihood, based not on charity but carnality, as he increased in stature both physically and in the eyes of the ladies? Or did despair-inducing poverty and the contempt of his wealthier compatriots drive him into a life of crime, perhaps imprisonment and premature death? With his good looks, quick mind, and ingratiating personality, I can see him today ensconced in one of those luxurious villas that cling to the hillside ringing the bay equally well as the kept consort of an aging American heiress, from whom he cajoles compensations as professionally as he conceals his contempt, or as the successful dealer in that illicit Mexican export with which Acapulco is linked in the clouded minds of its stoned American clientele. Whichever, or anywhere in between, I wish him well.

After a week in Acapulco I started getting antsy to move on, not knowing how long I had for my travels before the draft board caught up with me or how long the money would hold out. There was a lot more of Latin America to be seen, especially if we were to make it to Rio in time for Carnival. But Bill had gotten wrapped up in some surefire investment opportunity and was flying back and forth between Acapulco and Mexico City hammering out the details. He showed no inclination to be on his way. So it was decided I would drive the car down to the Mexico/Guatemala border by myself and Bill and Kathy would fly down and meet me there. We set a date a week hence when we would all rendezvous in the little Mexican border town of Tapachula.

Chapter 3 – TAPACHULA

I arrived in Tapachula after a week's swing through southern Mexico the day before the date set for my rendezvous with Bill and Kathy. The next morning I drove out to the airport to meet their flight, but no familiar faces descended from the plane. I called Bill and he told me negotiations were still ongoing, so they had to delay their departure from Acapulco a day. The next day, I trudged out to the airport once again; but again, no Bill and Kathy. Same routine the following day, and the day after that. Every day I'd call and every day Bill would assure me it would take just one more day to wrap up his wheeler-dealing

Unfortunately, Tapachula had considerably less to offer in the way of diversions than Acapulco. After a half-dozen frustrated trips to the airport, it was beginning to lose its charm. I had discovered one pastime, however, which filled a couple of hours a day pleasurably enough. This was the *paseo,* an evening ritual common to all Latin American towns in which the young people of the town promenade around the *plaza mayor,* the young ladies circling arm-in-arm in one direction while the young men - less affectionately but equally amiably - circle the other way. As they pass each other, longing gazes and coquettish remarks are exchanged. This was as close to a date as the young people in provincial, papist towns like Tapachula could aspire to. It was charming.

I enjoyed the spectacle from one of the benches that lined the parade route, being hesitant to *pasear* around the square myself for several reasons. One was that you got a longer look at the sashaying *señoritas* when you were stationary. That was enough of a reason right there, for the ladies dolled themselves up quite nicely. The amount of makeup the girls would cake on – sweet sixteen-year-olds who'd never been kissed were painted up like hookers are where I come from – took some getting used to, but that didn't take long since it was generally applied to good effect. To my bafflement, considering the conservative mores the *paseo* custom attested to, the young ladies were permitted to expose a surprising amount of bare flesh – this being the heyday of the mini-skirt, even in a town as remote from the fashion capitals of the world as Tapachula. I guess the thinking was there's nothing wrong with showing a little skin when it's so damn sure no young stud was going to get a chance to touch it.

Tapachula could not boast the abundance of beauties that a cosmopolitan place like Acapulco could, but there were a few who would stand out in any lineup. I remember one young lady in particular, who, without so much as uttering a word, provided me with a profound insight into Latin culture. She was the tallest of a threesome strolling arm in arm in the distaff direction. A sultry brunette of seventeen or eighteen with a stunning figure, her silken tresses were done up in the lion's mane style so popular with Latin girls at the time and still one of my favorites. The *de rigueur* heavy eye shadow, rouge, and lipstick took nothing away from her appearance, though it was unnecessary with her naturally luscious features – fine, arching eyebrows over flashing dark eyes, full ruby lips moist with sensuality, a *café con leche* complexion a bronzed goddess might envy.

True to my culture's taboo on staring, as well as my own timidity, I gave her only sidelong glances as she passed by me on her leisurely circuit. But my quick, inhibited looks were sufficient for me to see - with some surprise and even more delight - that she was staring unabashedly right at me as she passed, while whispering in the giggling, furtive manner of schoolgirls to her friends. She repeated the show of interest on each pass.

"Well," I thought, "If she wants it, I'm the one to give it to her."

So on the next pass, buoyed by my lusty fantasies, I plucked up my courage and gave her an eyeball-to-eyeball triple whammy back. The meaning of the salvo of ocular bombardment could not be mistaken: "'Well, baby, how 'bout it?'" To my surprise her reaction was not to smile or to wink but to blush deeply and rush off disconcerted with her friends, a look of embarrassed shock marring her pretty face. She never passed by me again.

I sat there feeling rather stupid, pondering the meaning of it all. I concluded that I, an obvious gringo, dressed in the dingiest way, must be something of a spectacle to the good people of Tapachula - perhaps one of those "hippies" from up north they'd heard about. The poor girl was just observing the freak show, totally innocent of the base desires she was capable of inspiring in one such as me. Here was a girl whose idea of naughty was probably sneaking out on the veranda for a quick kiss from her fiancé the night before her wedding, and I had virtually undressed her with my eyes right there in the town square. I felt like scum.

Much as the memory of my visual violation of that sweet thing haunts me even today, the experience did teach me two useful lessons. One was that a good Catholic, Latin girl, dressed, coiffured, and powdered like a harlot, is probably still a good Catholic girl. The other was that Latinos are not so hesitant to establish eye contact with strangers as we Americans, an eye contact lacking any deeper significance than curiosity. These lessons stood me in good stead throughout my travels in Latin America and beyond as I encountered other young ladies whose chastity was concealed behind a wanton allure and a provocative glance.

Tapachula opened my eyes to the charms of Latin women. Up until then I had restricted my gaze to the blond, modestly adorned *norteamericanas* I was familiar with. From then on, however, I never let a good-looking local girl pass by without a discreet but complete visual full body search. I loved the provocative way the Latin women dressed - each feminine curve accentuated - and their teasing, flirtatious mannerisms. I wondered how I'd overlooked them all those years growing up in Dallas. Perhaps my newly aroused appreciation simply resulted from the lack of suitable *gringas* in the places I dallied in, not from a broadening of my cultural horizon; but

I think not. I still find Latin women especially alluring. If only they weren't such good Catholics!

The one other pleasure I discovered in Tapachula was driving down to the little seaside town of Puerto Madero, half an hour away. Though they were in the same country and faced the same ocean, no two ports could be more different than Acapulco and Puerto Madero. No luxurious hotels or opulent villas here, just some rickety fishing shacks and a forlorn café with little to offer besides soda pop and Latin music blaring away at 180 decibels. No verdant, surrounding hills or breathtaking cliff views, just an uninterrupted panorama of mangrove swamps. But to my surprise, I found I liked Puerto Madero just as much as Acapulco, though for very different reasons.

With little else to do while waiting for my traveling companions to arrive, I would sit for hours on the thatch-shaded terrace of the café, reading a book, sipping Cokes, and wistfully gazing out over the azure expanse of the Pacific. Content with the tan I had acquired in Acapulco, I discovered the pleasure of sitting out of the sun, instead of in it, letting the gentle, tropical breeze refresh in a way air conditioning can never hope to duplicate. I concluded, with Kipling, that only mad dogs and Englishmen go out in the noonday sun, expanding the adage to include lotion-coated American tourists.

For mental stimulation, I cogitated on why the Coca-Cola in Mexico tasted so much better than what I was used to back home. I speculated it must be the water or some extra something the local bottler added to the recipe provided by Atlanta. Maybe it had to do with the way I was drinking it in those carefree days. With no urgent concerns to hurry to or flee from, I could savor it sip by casual sip, instead of guzzling it down to quench a thirst or wash down a Big Mac, as I was wont to do back home. Or it could have been the ambiance in which I usually enjoyed my Cokes in Mexico: out in the open air, under a blue tropical sky fringed with billowy white clouds, midst the splendor of exotic tropical flora. Or perhaps it was just nostalgia, the memories of home a Coke evoked. Whatever the reason, my impression of Coke's varietal nature was reinforced as I tasted of the vintages in countries all over the world in the years to come.

One day I forewent the trip to Puerto Madero to drive up into the mountains which rise lush and green behind Tapachula. I got lost on the rutted dirt roads and stopped to ask directions at an imposing house – mansion, you might say - out in the middle of nowhere. The neat rows of coffee trees stretching out in all directions and the tidy house and yard contrasted strikingly with the exuberant anarchy of the tropical forest I had been driving through all morning.

"*Perdona me*," I called to the woman tending the garden in front of the house, "*Puede dirigir me a Tapachula?*"

She stood up and I was surprised to see that she was tall and blond.

"Certainly," she responded in near accent-less English, "Just head back down the hill and when the road forks, take the fork to the left. Where are you coming from?"

"*De Estados Uni…* uh, from the United States." (I had been so intent on mustering up my meager command of the Spanish language, it took me a moment to realize I need suffer no further embarrassment.)

The lady, it turned out, was the wife of the manager of the place, the place being a huge coffee plantation, or "*finca*" as they are called down there, owned by German interests. She invited me in for coffee. In a little while we were joined by her husband, another tall, blond German, who walked in with the purposeful stride of someone who had more important things to do that day than entertain an itinerant American. He was cordial, nonetheless, and we all sat down to a relaxing cup of coffee and some biscuits.

Klaus and Ingrid both spoke excellent English. It was a treat chatting with them after hardly having spoken to anyone over the past week, and then only in broken Spanish. I think their cordiality sprang, in part, from a similar dearth of appropriate companionship. I marveled at their existence - two sophisticated, well-read Teutons jettisoned into a swarthy sea of Latino hired hands, some of whom I could see toiling away in the orchards below. Our similar cultural backgrounds created an instant bond, like that between ship passengers marooned on a desert island.

"So, how do you like Mexico?" Klaus asked, "God forsaken place, isn't it."

"It's a beautiful country," I ventured diplomatically, finding his assessment unnecessarily harsh. Lofty, snow-capped volcanoes towering over amber plains, palms leaning gracefully over the golden fringe of an azure sea, still nights filled with the sound of distant melodies was a curious way for God to forsake a place, I thought.

"Yes, it is, if you can stand the heat," Klaus countered, "and the Mexicans."

I was baffled by Klaus's hostility towards a country I considered one of the most beautiful I had been in and towards a people I had found uncommonly hospitable. I wondered what lay behind his attitude. I had found him very personable up to this point and been impressed with his cosmopolitan outlook on things. Now, disquieting undercurrents of an Aryan superiority complex entered my assessment of his personality. He looks like an *Übermensch*, I thought. Maybe he thinks he's one, too.

"They're really a worthless lot," Klaus went on without any need of encouragement. "The climate makes them lazy. If I weren't watching them all the time, nothing would get done. They'd be on siesta all the time."

"They're not all that way," Ingrid interjected. "I'd never be able to keep this house clean without Maria's help." ("Maria's our maid", she explained to me quickly as Klaus resumed his soliloquy.)

"Look what German ingenuity and drive have accomplished" – this with a sweep of his arm over the neat rows of coffee trees extending down the hillside – "If we left, the whole thing would revert to jungle within a generation."

I wanted to ask Klaus what he thought the climate was like when the ancestors of these lethargic Mexicans had built Tenochtitlan and the other wondrous ruins I had visited recently. Or point out that while his energetic Germans had supplied the capital and organization that made the *finca* the impressive enterprise it was, it was these "lazy" Mexicans who had done all the dirty work. But I refrained out of politeness, or wimpiness, perhaps. The *finca* was, in truth, a tribute to somebody's skill and industriousness. And I wasn't the one responsible for getting the Mexicans to pick coffee beans in hundred-degree heat.

I puzzled over Klaus's attitude as I drove back to Tapachula. He seemed like a goodhearted, intelligent person, but I couldn't accept his evaluation of the Mexicans. Sure, they appeared to be lazy if you judged by the throngs of languid men loitering on street corners or sitting in cafes drinking and chatting for hours on end. But I attributed their behavior to a different worldview. They had not been inculcated from birth, like Klaus and me, with the artificial needs of our industrialized world – a bigger house, a newer car, the need to make one's mark. Their needs were more elemental – a roof over their heads, enough food for the kids, some security against tomorrow – and the simplicity of their needs enabled them to retain their perspective, to avoid the mistake of subordinating to a craving for material possessions what was really important: their relations with their fellow man.

Perhaps I was being romantic, or over indulgent. In any case, Klaus's perspective was one I was to encounter over and over again in the ensuing years. At first it just bothered me as not being very nice; eventually, when I understood it better and had observed some of its unfortunate consequences, I came to despise it as ignorantly narrow-minded and unjustifiably and unbearably smug.

Bill and Kathy continued to miss the daily plane from Acapulco and "just one more day" had now become a week. So, after one last hopeful trip to the airport ended in disappointment, I left the car in the parking lot with a note telling them I was going to hitchhike through Central America and would meet them in Panama City in a week. I suggested the local American Express office as our point of contact.

Chapter 4 – GUATEMALA

Before I left Texas I never would have guessed that you could hitchhike through Central America, but in traveling around Mexico I had met people who had done it. It sounded cheap, easy, and a lot of fun. The ease with which I caught rides across Guatemala verified what I had been told. Vehicles were not that numerous, even on the Pan American Highway, but those which did happen along were as likely as not to stop and see what that gawky *gringo* standing by the side of the road with his thumb out wanted. But I made two mistakes at the beginning of my foray, one of which had repercussions so long as I was in Spanish-speaking countries, the other of which was somewhat amusingly rectified a few days later.

We had two books in the car: a Spanish grammar and Arthur Frommer's *Latin America On $5 a Day*. I felt I was entitled to one of them for the delay Bill had forced on me, frittering away my precious, pre-induction days of travel. Stupidly, I chose the Frommer book. As it turned out, $5 a day was way above what I could afford - or needed to spend - in my travels through Latin America. I really could have used that Spanish grammar, though.

My second mistake I didn't discover until I reached the border between Guatemala and El Salvador.

"*No puede pasar*," the Guatemalan border official informed me.

"*Por que?*" I asked, anxious to be on my way as it was mid-afternoon and I wanted to make San Salvador, the capital, before nightfall.

"*No tiene prueba de entrada*", he explained, deadpan.

It seems I had neglected to get my passport stamped when I entered Guatemala from Mexico and the Guatemalan border officials wouldn't let me out of the country without the requisite imprint. I remembered the border crossing just outside Tapachula well. Sure, there was a building on the Guatemala side that looked governmental and had something official-looking written over the door, but nobody directed me into it and I couldn't read the sign. I assumed all borders were like the one between Mexico and the United States, where you can just walk across and amble on down the road – at least if you look American and are headed in the right direction. So that's what I did. What I was supposed to do was go inside that building and get my passport stamped, proving I had entered the country.

I tried to reason with border agent, arguing that my presence standing before him proved I had entered the country and all I wanted to do was leave it, for which Guatemala would no doubt be the better. To no avail. He insisted I had to return to Guatemala City, the capital, and have my passport stamped at the *Ministerio des Relaciones Extranjeros*. I don't know what would have happened had I tried to bribe him, but that stereotypical approach to Latin officialdom never occurred to me. With my thin wallet, he probably would have just laughed at whatever gratuity I offered.

I was fuming. On the advice of a Guatemalan - well-meaning, but ignorant of the exigencies of hitchhiking - I had turned off the PanAm and taken a back road to the border. It had taken me three hours to cover the 50 or so miles from Guatemala City, and in the half hour I'd been at the border post I hadn't seen anything cross the bridge which spanned the river delineating the border in either direction. The thought occurred to me that this border crossing was reminiscent in its casualness to the one by which I'd entered the country.

"Well," I thought to myself, "I just walked into this country. Maybe I can just walk out."

I started nonchalantly ambling toward the bridge and had almost reached my goal when a soldier popped out of the bushes and blocked my way with his rifle across my chest.

"*No puede pasar*," he said. I knew what that meant now; I'd heard it before.

I thought this young man, being about my age, might be more reasonable than his superior. He looked more bemused than hostile. So, in the dozen or so words of Spanish I could muster, I tried to explain my predicament and begged him to let me cross. He continued to shake his head, but with a smile that suggested a friendly attitude. After laughing a bit at my feeble attempts to communicate, he took me aside in a conspiratorial way and through gestures and real slow Spanish made me understand that back up the road a hundred yards or so was a path through the woods down to the river. He was suggesting I take the path and just wade across the border.

Sounded too simple to me and too much like an actual criminal act, but I was desperate. I decided to try it. With a wink to my fellow conspirator I turned around and headed back up the road. I found the path easily enough; it looked better traveled than the official route across the border.

"Lots of people forget to get their passports stamped it appears," I mused.

The path led me right down to the river's edge as promised. I took off my shoes, socks, and jeans and was about to step into the swiftly flowing river, which appeared about waist deep, when I noticed a woman on the far bank who was washing her clothes in the stream signaling to me to walk upstream a ways. She seemed to be indicating a better place to cross.

"Another indication crossing the border this way is not all that unusual," I chuckled to myself.

Halfway across the stream a chilling thought hit me. What if the border guard was setting me up? What if he just wanted to take a potshot at me as I crossed the river so he could get credit for bagging a wetback – a *gringo* at that! I jerked around apprehensively and looked up towards the bridge where I had encountered the guard. He was standing there nonchalantly smoking a cigarette, while watching my progress across the stream. When he saw me looking his way, he gave me a little smile and a covert thumbs up.

When I got to the other side, a truck full of *campesinos* was starting across the bridge into El Salvador. I knew I should go down to the Salvadoran border station to get my passport stamped so I wouldn't face the same problem when I left El Salvador, but that truck was the only vehicle I'd seen since getting to the border and I didn't want to miss it. I raced up the hill to the road and caught my ride into San Salvador, where I immediately reported to the Ministry of Foreign Relations. I made up some cock and bull story as to why I didn't have an entry stamp in my passport and after some skeptical shaking of heads they granted me the coveted stamp, with the proviso that I be out of El Salvador within three days. Looking around San Salvador I decided that was two days more than I needed, and the next morning found me crossing into Honduras in the approved manner. I never blew a border crossing again.

Chapter 5 – CANAL ZONE

I got to Panama City on the day appointed for my rendezvous with Bill and Kathy but they never showed. I left a note for them at American Express. It was still there when I left Panama a few days later. I wasn't too broken up about failing to reunite with them. I missed the company (There were days when I didn't speak a word to anyone, or, if I did, only in Spanish), but I'd found that I preferred my new mode of travel. It was a better way to meet the local folk, and they'd proven very hospitable. I'd been treated to numerous meals and had usually been offered a place to sleep, so I didn't much miss my bedroom-on-wheels.

Our trip would probably have ended here, anyway. In our limited pre-departure research we had overlooked the Darien Gap. This miasma of swamps and jungle between Panama City and Colombia is so impenetrable the Pan American Highway had not yet been cut through it (It still hasn't). So, we would have had to ship the car to Cali, Colombia or give up. I was sure Bill would opt for the latter.

Panama City was my first mail drop since leaving home. Waiting for me at American Express were a number of letters from my family and one ominously marked "U.S. Government - Official Business". It was, as I suspected, notice from my draft board that I had been reclassified 1-A.

"Oh well", I consoled myself, "I've still got a little time." I didn't know where exactly I was headed after Panama other than my final destination of Rio de Janeiro, so I gave that to my family as my next mailing address.

It was Christmas Eve and what with the season and the letters from home I was feeling very homesick, very lonely. I envisioned the dinner my six brothers and sisters and their families would be sharing about that exact time. I missed them, but in my self-centeredness it never occurred to me how much they must be worried about me. Little did I know how many Christmases would pass before I would be joining them singing carols round the Christmas tree once again.

Panama City did nothing to relieve my depression. It was dirty and crowded and smelled of haphazardly disposed of garbage and a faulty sewer system. I passed shoddy wooden tenements which appeared to have been built back in the 1910s to house the workers who dug the Panama Canal. Almost all the original paint had peeled off the walls, the balconies sagged, the railings were all askew. They would have been condemned as uninhabitable long ago back in the States. Whole families were living six to eight to a room.

"These people's grandparents lived in these when they were new," I reflected, "Now their descendants still live in them, only they aren't so nice any more." I questioned whether the average Panamanian was better off now than back then.

Finding it all too depressing, I took refuge in the Canal Zone, hoping to find there a familiar environment which might offer some relief from my loneliness. Once I was through the heavily guarded main gate (the sentries let me through without even asking for an ID, so much was I obviously one of them), I wasn't disappointed. Primly maintained buildings graced neatly trimmed lawns on which kids clad in cut-offs tossed frisbees back and forth.

"Replace the palm trees with loblolly pine", I said to myself, "and this could be an army base in Georgia."

On a corner of the main square was a PX-like company store that carried everything from peanut butter and Hostess twinkies to our type of football - oblong instead of round. A snack shop offered that pinnacle of American *haute cuisine*: hamburgers.

I ordered burger and a chocolate shake and sat down at a formica-topped table. While I waited for my order, I noticed I was getting sidelong glances from the other Americans present. I wondered why as I felt like I blended in perfectly. Sure, I was scraggly but so were all the other young people around. Then it dawned on me that while we were all scruffy, they were clean scruffy, not dirty scruffy like me. Their jeans were faded but not filthy, their hair unkempt but not matted. When the couple at the next table got up and moved to another table, I sensed there might be an olfactory difference between myself and my fellow Americans as well.

"Hmmm, maybe it's time to do some laundry," I concluded, "And get a shower."

The hamburger tasted like ambrosia, the shake like nectar; I'd missed them so. Sated and feeling like I'd just had Christmas dinner - and not a bad one at that - I inquired about a laundromat and headed off to where I was directed. A sign on the door, however, indicated the facility was closed due to a power outage.

"Out again, huh," a stocky, thirtyish gentleman standing behind me with a pillow-cased bundle over his shoulder said, "Second time this week. Oh well, I only came over here because the machine in our building is tied up. Guess I'll just have to wait my turn. Care to join me?"

"Thanks," I replied, grateful for the company as much as for the assistance.

Larry Patterson — that was his name — taught music at the Canal Zone school and lived with his wife and infant son in one of the comfortable-looking apartment blocks which lined the square. When he learned I was a homeless waif, he invited me to join him and his family for Christmas dinner. He tactfully mentioned I could use his shower if I wanted to. I got the hint and took him up on his offer when we got back to his place. Showered and shaved, with clean clothes to wear, and finding Larry and his wife, Mary, very pleasant and gracious hosts, I felt like this might not be such a bad Christmas after all.

The Patterson's had decorated their apartment in the spirit of the season as best they could, festooning the living room with the traditional accoutrements of Christmas. A small tropical pine tree strung with lights stood in a corner. On a table a plastic Santa and his reindeer rode over white and crunchy snow simulated with cotton tuffs. Three stockings hung from a bookcase, used in lieu of a mantle.

"We do this for our son's sake mostly," Larry remarked, "It's hard for Mary and I to get into the Christmas spirit with the air conditioner on and the bougainvillea in bloom. We come from North Dakota, you know."

I had to agree, though I thought the hospitality they extended to me was a pretty good imitation of the kindness we associate with the season. I wish I'd told them so.

"Look at this," Larry went on, picking up a package from under the tree. "It's a present for my son from his grandmother. Same thing every year – woolen mittens. She's lived in North Dakota all her life and can't imagine a place where you don't need these things in the wintertime. Same thing when we were living in Samoa. We tried to explain to hear the first couple of years, but now we just send her a thank you note."

"You know it's just her way of telling you it's time to come home," Mary shouted from the kitchen. I could imagine the note that kind soul would send to her mother-in-law: "Thanks for the lovely mittens. They're just what Johnny needed."

I ended up spending the night with the Pattersons. The next day Larry gave me a tour of the canal. From a point overlooking the manmade waterway we watched the massive locks being opened and closed as a freighter was lifted to the level of Gatun Lake.

"Magnificent, isn't it," Larry observed, "Makes you proud to be an American, doesn't it."

"Yes, it does," I replied.

"You know the Panamanians want to take it over," Larry remarked.

I'd seen the political slogans all over Panama City, ineffectively painted over so their message that the *Yanquis* in the Canal Zone should rejoin their families back home – and *pronto!* - was still decipherable. There had been riots recently.

"I sometimes wonder how I would feel if I lived on their side of the fence," Larry went on. "The Panamanians are always pointing out what an unfair lease we imposed on their fledgling country and reminding us it was their fathers and grandfathers, for the most part, who died building the Canal. I suppose they're right that the lease wouldn't stand up in an American court of law. It is their country's only real asset, but it's hard to be sympathetic when they're throwing rocks and burning cars right outside the gate."

"I can imagine," I said, though I really couldn't, not being directly involved in or even familiar with the controversy. I didn't know where I stood on the issue. I think I pretty much didn't care one way or the other. But I respected Larry for his attempt to see both sides of the question. Most people on either side of the fence were not so open-minded.

The next day I booked a seat on a flight to Bogota, grumbling about the $75 I had to shell out for the ticket. I had considered hiking the 80 or so miles through the Darien Gap to Colombia. I'd heard it could be done. But when Larry told me about the two American kids who got lost in the jungle behind their house and been found the next morning dead, their bodies swollen with mosquito bites, I decided flying was the more prudent option.

Chapter 6 – THE PANAM

The next month and a half I spent wending my way down the west coast of South America, mostly along the Pan American Highway. I hitched most of the way, occasionally needing to shell out for a boat, train, or bus to cross some unbridgeable gap, like the Gulf of Guayaquil, or to get through some nether stretch where the traffic - always light - dwindled away to nothing but donkeys and pedestrians. I met lots of friendly people – from *campesinos* to oligarchs – and partook of much good-hearted hospitality, often from folks who could little afford it. I'd marveled at wonders - scenic and cultural – as remarkable as anything I had seen in my travels in Europe. I learned a lot but could have learned a lot more, had I opted for that Spanish grammar instead of Mr. Frommer.

In the fifty or so days I'd been on the road without my handy bedroom-on-wheels I had been forced to sleep out in some field or dark corner only half a dozen times. I'd paid for accommodations in hotels - none of which were elegant enough to make Frommer's - a like number of times. The rest of the time I had found a place to stay. "Found" is not exactly accurate as more often than not a place to stay found me. Latin culture seemed designed to cater to the needs of a vagabond such as myself, though one Latin custom worked against me. If someone picked me up and we stopped to eat, his conception of hospitality required him to pay for my meal. I suspect I missed many rides because of this obligation. As a meal was not nearly as critical to me as a ride, I felt like holding up a sign saying "All I want is a ride. You don't have to feed me!"

Foremost amongst the Latin customs in usefulness to me was the *paseo*. I would take a seat on a bench in the plaza in whatever town I had reached that day. My lanky, blondish, fair-eyed physiognomy left little doubt as to where I hailed from; the backpack by my side, little doubt as to what I was doing. Soon I would be surrounded by a host of young people, staring at me in a curious but friendly way while several of the bolder ones asked me questions simultaneously. It was as if the circus had come to town.

When they learned I had no place to stay the night, one of my interlocutors might invite me to his home, but more often they would lead me off to the village priest, the local Peace Corps volunteer, or whatever fellow *gringo* might reside in the town. There I invariably found lodgings. I sort of dreaded it when a fellow American, like Larry Patterson, asked, "Where are you staying?" It put them in the uncomfortable position of either ungraciously changing the subject or offering me a place to stay. To my credit, I humbly submit, I never once asked anyone for a place to stay; I always let them make the offer. But I realized my mode of travel created a situation in which they couldn't very well not make the offer, no matter how much of an imposition I might be. I felt like a moocher. It was different when the local people offered me a place to stay. Then I didn't feel so bad. I felt I earned my keep through the entertainment value, as well as by giving them a chance to practice their English.

I had a lot of respect for the Peace Corps volunteers I encountered in tiny, remote villages where they were the only English-speakers in town and the only thing to do on a Saturday night was to write doleful letters home. I wondered if I could last a year or two in such a place. It would certainly have tried my patience and my dedication. The volunteers I met in the cities or traveling about on trains a class higher than I could afford I had less respect for. Those guys I figured were just draft dodgers like myself. You could usually get a deferment if you joined the Corps, though the Selective Service left it up to the local draft boards whether to grant deferments or not (My board, true to the red-white-and-blue, super-patriotism my hometown is famous for, chose not to). Of course, a draft deferment is not what motivated the gals. I'm not sure what did. I don't know what the ratio of men to women in the Corps was back then, but maybe it was seen as a good husband hunting ground by less comely birds of prey ("Birds" was a British term for chicks in vogue at the time). Or maybe they really were motivated by the idealism the Corps espoused.

I found the philosophy behind the Corps unappealing, smacking too much of the White Man's Burden. How it worked out in practice fed my contempt. Most of the volunteers seemed to be liberal arts majors like myself. What did these spoiled brats of a consumptive society, with their degrees in English literature, Art History, and the like, think they had to teach Latinos who had learned to survive, with great ingenuity and resourcefulness, under conditions which would drive most of us to despair? The Corps would wax lyrical over some oft-told success story – the volunteer in *Barrio Impoverisado* who had taught the natives to make fuel efficient stoves out of old coffee cans or some such triumph of American ingenuity. What nonsense! I scorned them for their pretentious, self-congratulatory air. The ones with the poster of Che Guevara on the wall I found especially hard to take, their revolutionary posturing being blatantly faddish and insincere. I suspected a few years later most of them would be working on Wall Street (Of course, I refrained from expressing my opinion while partaking of their food or bedding down on their couch). I felt vindicated in my critique when in later years the Peace Corps put more emphasis on recruiting those with solid technical expertise and utilized the liberal arts types for something they were good at: teaching English.

People often ask me if I wasn't scared traveling the way I did. At first I was, when sleeping out in some isolated spot or climbing into a truck full of swarthy, unshaven, semi-inebriated *campesinos* in the middle of the night. I remember being a little frightened when I woke up from sleeping under a bush on the outskirts of San Salvador and found a somnolent, down-and-out soul under every bush around. I wondered if they might have done me harm if my sleeping bag hadn't concealed my ethnicity and made me look like all the other penniless bums. But I soon came to realize that anyone who picked me up, being the owner of a car, pickup, or truck, was so well-off by local standards he wasn't likely to risk it all by molesting me.

Moreover, Latin America seemed to be free of the senseless, random violence which plagues our society. I felt safer hitchhiking down there than I would have walking the streets of many cities back home.

The only real scary moment of the trip so far came not from the threat of violence but from the condition of the roads and the driving habits of the locals. I was working my way down from Lima to Cuzco by the Andean route and the sparseness of the traffic caused me to pay a fare to ride in the back of a truck for the final leg from Abancay to Cuzco. I spread my sleeping bag on top of the enormous bundles of coca leaves my traveling companions - mostly Quechua Indian women - had hefted onto the truck (I never saw any Indian men toiling under such loads, only the women). Having secured my room for the night, I settled back to enjoy the scenery, which was spectacular (The Andes making the Rockies look like foothills).

On the side of the truck I had made my bed on the mountainside dropped precipitously off to some barely discernible stream thousands of feet below. Above us the mountains rose up so high their tops could not be seen. The hillsides were brilliant shades of green, with colorful, caped shepherds – tiny in the distance - tending their flocks of llamas in stone-rimmed pastures. The picturesqueness was completed by the winding, narrow, cobbled road we bounced along, built by the Incas and better maintained in their day than in ours.

As night fell we stopped for a pee break and all the men, including myself, hopped down to answer the call. For some reason the women stayed on the truck. Quechua women are the most sexless creatures I have ever seen, with their squat bodies swaddled in numerous petticoats and sweaters, their heads topped by incongruous, unfeminine bowler hats.

"Maybe their bladder control is just another sign of their lack of femininity," I speculated, "Or maybe they pee in their panties. With all those petticoats no one would ever know."

KEN KIASK

Whatever the case, the men all squatted down female-style while they did their business, whether because they are as feminine as their women are masculine or to protect the modesty of the dainty Indian maidens I couldn't say. I did my business in my accustomed, upright posture, figuring the darkness hid any sight of that which might offend, and chuckled to myself, looking at the men and remembering the boast of one of my fraternity brothers that he would "screw anything that squats to piss."

I climbed back onto the truck, snuggled down in my sleeping bag, and, properly relieved, dozed off. I woke up in the middle of the night with a tremendous urge to pee. It had started to rain and the truckers had spread a tarp across the back of the truck without even waking me. The coca bag on which I lay elevated me so high that the tarp pressed tight against my sleeping bag, which was not waterproof. I was soaking wet and cold. Moreover, I couldn't move except for a slight turning of my head. I looked down to where a corner of the tarp flapped loosely as we jostled along. I could see about a foot's width of cobblestones beyond which there was nothing but a black abyss. If one wheel slipped off the bumpy road, there was nothing to stop our descent till we splattered into the river far below.

Music blared from the cab where the driver was stuffed in along with three or four of his compatriots. I knew from previous experience they were more than likely passing around a bottle of *aguardiente*, the local firewater made from sugarcane, the driver only sporadically interrupting his gesticulation-punctuated yakking to cast a cursory glance at the road ahead. I could see the filler in the *Dallas Morning News* the next day with the only sort of news we seemed to get about Latin America back then:

Truck Plunges Off Andean Highway, 11 Killed

ABANCAY, PERU – A truck carrying 12 persons careened off the main road to Cuzco last night, plunging two thousand feet down the mountainside into the rain swollen waters of the Apurimac River. All aboard were killed except the driver

30

who was found wandering around in a daze, the top half of a broken bottle, from which he continued to try and drink, clutched in his hand. One passenger, who appeared to be a drug smuggler from the many coca leaves pressed into his flattened body, reflected how harrowing the fall must have been, being found in a puddle of his own urine.

I wondered how long it would be before my family found out who the drug smuggler was.

With the cold, the wet, the need to pee, the stark terror of impending death, I spent an uncomfortable, terrified, sleepless night. When we pulled - still alive - into Cuzco with the dawn's first light, I jumped down from the truck and just about kissed the ground before running off to find a bathroom. I treated myself to one of my infrequent hotel stays that night. I felt I'd earned it.

Chapter 7 – PUERTO MONTT

The problem wasn't that I didn't have any money. I still had about a hundred of the three hundred dollars I'd left Dallas with. The problem was that the money I had wasn't in exchangeable form. I had put off cashing a traveler's check in hopes my remaining Chilean escudos would hold out until I crossed the border into Argentina. I was trying to save the dollar or so I would lose on the exchange rate if I changed a traveler's check into escudos, then exchanged whatever escudos I had left when I left the country into Argentine pesos.

When I reached Puerto Montt, I had 25 centavos left. I realized I would have to cash a check to get to the border. I was in the Chilean Lake District. I had to take a bus to a lake, then a ferry across the lake, then another bus to a lake in Argentina. I went to a bank only to discover that it was a national holiday. It was Friday and the bank wouldn't reopen until Monday. Carnival was fast approaching so I didn't want to wait till then, but no other place in town would cash a traveler's check.

My immediate needs were taken care of when I met some American fellow wanderers who invited me to sleep on their floor and shared with me their bedtime snack of tea and cookies, it being well past the dinner hour. Lying in my sleeping bag on the un-posturepedic floor, I pondered what to do on the morrow but could not come up with a solution. It was too far to walk to the first lake and, even if I did, I couldn't very well swim across it.

In the morning I headed down to the bus station to see what fate might bring. When I arrived at the station, the bus to the lake, crammed with Chilean and foreign tourists, was just about to pull out. Desperate to be on it, I hopped on and tried to explain my predicament to the driver, hoping one of us would come up with a solution. I wasn't making much headway, either because my Spanish was incomprehensible or because the driver didn't like what he was hearing.

"Pardon me," someone interrupted us from behind, "Can I be of some help?" It was a young Chilean with an engaging smile and excellent English.

I explained my situation to him and he turned and spoke to the driver. I could tell from his tone and see by the driver's reaction that he was a persuasive talker, though I didn't have a clue what he was saying. After a minute or two of conversation the driver motioned to me to take a seat. I settled in with Pablo – that was my savior's name – and his friends. They were all Chilean university students who were touring the Lake District over their summer vacation (January being summer down there). We chatted amiably as the bus whizzed us to our destination. I also met an elderly British couple on the bus whom I hit up for the fare across the lake, promising to repay them when we got to Argentina.

We spent the night between the two lakes, the well-heeled older tourists staying at the rustic but grand hotel, while Pablo, his friends, and I found accommodations in a big room over the border police station. They shared their provisions with me; then, the night being cold, we gathered round the wood stove to drink our after-dinner tea and chat. The subject soon turned to politics.

"You are a spy, aren't you?" Antonio blurted out suddenly. He was the only one of the group who hadn't been entirely friendly to me since I boarded the bus. I noticed him during the day standing aside, sullenly giving me sidelong glances.

"For whom?" I asked quite innocently. The question caught me totally off-guard and I really didn't know whom he had in mind.

"The CIA," he replied with a sneer. I'd heard of them but wasn't sure exactly what they did.

"No, I'm not," I stated firmly, bemused to think how chagrined Antonio would feel if he knew my real relationship with my government at that moment

"I don't believe you," he snarled and with that withdrew himself to a far corner of the room.

"You'll have to excuse Antonio," Pablo explained. "He's hotheaded and suspicious of everyone, but his intentions are good."

"And what intentions are those?" I asked forcefully, my blood rising now from having been accused of ulterior purposes by someone I had been nothing but friendly with. I really resented his breaking up the convivial atmosphere like that.

"To help his people," Pablo replied matter of factly.

"Oh," I uttered, somewhat mollified, "But why would he think I was a spy?"

"They do exist, you know."

"That's true," I granted. I knew we had them; I knew the Soviet Union had them. Britain had one famous, fictional one and probably more. But I couldn't imagine what they would be doing way down here in Chile.

"But what would they be doing in Chile?' I asked, converting my thoughts into words.

"Protecting American interests," Pablo responded without hesitation and again very matter of factly.

"How do they do that?"

"Oh, they fund political parties; they bribe government officials; they infiltrate radical movements like the one we are all engaged in."

"To what end?" I asked, still not getting it.

"To protect American interests," Pablo repeated patiently, as if instructing a dullard. "In Chile, that would be, first and foremost, the copper mines."

I had passed the huge Chiquicamata mine on the train ride from Bolivia down to the coast in Chile. I knew it was owned by the American company, Anaconda. I assumed they weren't running it as a charitable enterprise. So at least Anaconda had a vested interest in Chile.

"But I thought those mines were a tremendous boost to the Chilean economy. I've heard the companies pay their workers well above the average wage."

"Those wages are a reflection of the excess profits the American companies are taking out of our country. It keeps the workers loyal."

"I suppose that could be true," I conceded.

"For years we have been trying to take over the mines so that we could gain all the profits from our most important natural resource and use them to the benefit of Chile. What do you suppose would happen if we ever succeeded?"

"I don't know," I admitted, and I really didn't. I knew what Klaus would have said: "Those mines wouldn't be anything but big holes in the ground within a generation!"

"The three or four companies which control the international trade in copper," Pablo went on, answering his own question, "would refuse to buy our copper. Your government would probably impose an embargo on us, as it did on Cuba when Castro nationalized the sugar plantations, gambling casinos, and other American holdings. Those spies, whose existence you seem to doubt, would try to topple the government which had done it, and, Chile being as weak and corrupt as it is, they probably would succeed."

"Sounds a little paranoid to me," I ventured, hoping Pablo would not be offended as his attitude towards me, despite the nasty machinations he was attributing to my government, continued to be friendly.

"Does it? You passed through Panama on your way down here, did you not? You know how you won the concession to build the canal, don't you?"

"Sure," I said. But despite a major in American history all I could remember was that Panama won its independence from Colombia and shortly thereafter we were granted the concession.

"You didn't like the terms Colombia demanded for the right to build the canal," he continued, mercifully sparing me from having to give my sketchy recollection of the sequence of events. "So you fomented a revolt by the Panamanians. Then you landed marines in Panama to prevent Colombia from putting down the revolt. No sooner had the independence of the country been declared than you recognized the new rulers, and a few days after that you had your concession under the terms you wanted."

"The Panamanians don't seem to be very grateful for the help we gave them in winning their independence these days. They seem to think they got a raw deal, too."

"Yes, they do. All of us Latin Americans think we have gotten a raw deal, as you call it, from your country for a long time."

"Well, you don't see us landing the Marines these days," I pointed out.

"Oh really! And just what were those heavily armed amphibians who emerged out of the water in the Dominican Republic in 1965."

I'd forgotten about that. In fact, it had barely intruded on my consciousness when it happened. The official rationale must have been something like "to restore law and order", but I didn't dare raise that with this crowd!

"But you're right," Pablo went on, "Military interventions are only a final resort and are seldom needed to maintain control these days. Imperialism works in more subtle ways today, but its motives remain the same. Unfortunately, our ability to fight back has not improved much since the Colombians were forced to accept the dismemberment of their country."

I snickered inside at his use of the word "imperialism". We had given up our empire long ago when we granted the Philippines their independence. I was tempted to ask him whether he considered Puerto Rico, the Virgin Islands, Guam, and American Samoa an empire but deferred out of politeness. Weeks later, at a library maintained by the United States Information Agency (USIA), I checked out his interpretation of how we had gained the Canal Zone and found his narrative much closer to the facts than my own glossing-over understanding.

"But why can't you fight back," I asked, truly curious, "You have your own government, your own army."

Pablo smiled patronizingly. "You don't understand the social dynamics within our country. It's difficult to explain but let me give you an example. When we buy tractors to mechanize our agriculture, you consider it a sign of 'development'. If your Agency for International Development or the World Bank, which you control, provides funds to subsidize the purchase of these tractors, you take pride in your benevolence."

"Of course, they must be overpriced American tractors we are forced to buy," someone in the group interjected.

"But what happens to these tractors? Our *campesinos* can't use them. Their farms are too small. They can't even afford the gas. One way or another, they end up in the hands of our rich landowners. And what do they use them for? To improve the country's ability to feed itself? No, they use them to grow crops for export. And what happens to the foreign exchange they earn? Does it go to building up our economy? Some perhaps, but too much is used to buy imported luxury items or is invested in condominiums in Miami or is stashed away in Swiss banks as a safeguard against the day when the privileged lose their privileges because of their unpatriotic deeds."

"If this were all, it might not be so bad, but it gets worse. What happens to our *campesinos* and their little farms? If they are just tenants on land owned by the rich landowner, they get kicked off the land because their landlord can make more profitable use of it now growing export crops with his new tractors. Even if he owns his own farm, the *campesino* may be dependent on wages he earns working for the rich landowner part-time to supplement his meager income. But the rich landowner no longer needs that many *campesinos*. His new tractors can do the work of hundreds of men. So the *campesino* gets poorer and poorer and eventually is forced to sell his land to the rich landowner. Sometimes the landowner acquires the land by more direct and forceful means, illegal even in our oligarchy-controlled country. What does the land-less, unemployed *campesino* do? He moves his family to the city, the only place there is the hope of work, where he lives in shanty towns with all the other displaced *campesinos*, eking out an existence through the occasional odd job or the 'charity' of the same rich who made his life miserable in the first place."

"But what about our rich landowners? Are they not concerned about their fellow citizens? They're so wrapped up in their foreign sports cars or the latest fashions from Paris or trips to Las Vegas that they aren't even aware of ther plight, much like the way many of you Americans aren't aware of the life the blacks in your ghettos live. They send their kids off to America to be educated and they come back having more in common with you Americans than they do with their fellow countrymen. They get their opinions and facts from *Time* magazine and American 'experts', so that when they buy a shiny new tractor, or receive one as 'foreign aid', they think, like you Americans, that they are contributing to their country's development. If any of them are perceptive enough to see what's really going on, they are faced with the choice of joining us in the movement - and facing the ostracism of their class and perhaps imprisonment - or turning in fear to the army to protect their property and their lifestyle."

"And what about our army, trained by you, armed by you, indoctrinated by you? Are they not concerned about the fate of their country? You guess! They're so brainwashed by your anticommunist dogma, which fits so well the generals' own position in society, they wrap themselves in a banner of traditional values - Family, God, Country - and label anyone who questions the status quo a subversive. No wonder the weapons they seek from you - and you are only too willingly to provide - are those they can use, not against an external enemy, but against the very people they have sworn to defend."

"So what about our country as a whole? Is it better or worse off from the mechanization of our agriculture? Because more and more of our land is dedicated to the growing of crops for export, we find we cannot feed ourselves. We must use our precious foreign exchange, which should be going to build up our infrastructure, to buy imported foodstuffs."

"Food for Peace!" someone shouted out and the whole group laughed. I didn't get the joke. Later, when I began to look into some of the issues raised by this chat, I learned that the "Food for Peace" program had initially been called simply "Public Law 480". It had been passed by Congress as a law "for the promotion of American agriculture." Under P.L. 480, the government buys surplus production from our farmers and sells it to other countries at a discount. If this concerned manufactured goods, not agricultural produce, it would be called "dumping", a nasty practice against which elaborate mechanisms have been put in place to see that no one is tempted to try it. Many recipients of our dumped agricultural surplus, or "Food for Peace" if you will, have found it to be a Trojan Horse which has thwarted the development of their own agriculture and increased their dependence on imported food. I found it reprehensible that we tried to dress up a program primarily designed for our own benefit with such a hokey, self-serving name.

"So," Pablo concluded, repeating his earlier question, "Is our country better or worse off from the mechanization of our agriculture?"

"It's hard to say," I responded unsurely. I still believed the tremendous increase in production mechanization brought was bound to be a good thing in the long run. It had worked for us, after all.

"It *is* hard to say," Pablo agreed. "That's why we want a system which will guarantee that all the benefits of mechanization go to the building up of our country and that all share equitably in those benefits. That's what we are striving for."

Pablo was exhausted by his harangue. He had delivered it not in the smooth-flowing English in which I have recounted it - his English was good but not that good – but in a halting, stutter-step way, groping for the right word and frequently needing to rephrase his remarks to make himself clear. It was now late, so we all decided to turn in. As I crawled into my sleeping bag, Antonio came by and apologized. I think he had been impressed by the open-minded and sincerely inquisitive way I had listened to Pablo's speech. Then, when the lights went out, Pablo, who was lying next to me, leaned over and asked, in a soft, almost pleading voice, "You will think over what we have talked about tonight, won't you?" I promised him I would.

And I did, the very next day, as I trudged up the winding dirt road that led over the crest of the Andes - here only two thousand feet high - to Argentina. I had decided to walk the fifteen miles between the two lakes, not wanting to be indebted to yet another generous soul for the bus fare. The ferry across the Argentine lake was scheduled to leave at noon, so I had gotten up early and was making good progress.

Or so I thought as I stood straddling the continental divide, relieved that the uphill part of the trek was behind me. Then I heard the sound of the bus bringing the other tourists laboring up the hill. I put on my most forlorn look, hoping the driver would be so moved by my rain-soaked, tired appearance that he would stop and give me a lift the rest of the way. Swoosh! The bus roared past me without so much as a wave.

"I'd better get moving," I advised myself and set off at a quickened pace. I walked and walked, but each time I rounded a bend, expecting to see the lake with the ferryboat moored to its slip, all I saw was another bend in the road further on. I began to get worried I might miss the boat, so I picked up the pace, starting to trot. I became increasingly anxious as bend followed bend with no sign of the lake. I was contemplating jettisoning some of my cargo, like the crumbled sport coat I'd dragged all the way down the continent without ever wearing, when the lake suddenly came into view a few hundred yards down the road. The ferry was still there, loaded with passengers and apparently about to depart. I sprinted the last hundred yards and was on the dock when a voice from behind me shouted "*Pare!* (Halt!)".

I turned and saw a uniformed official waving me back. I had forgotten this was the border and ran back to the border post to get my passport stamped. As the official began with the formalities I tried to explain to him that I had to catch that ferry. He proceeded with a deliberate slowness which to me indicated he couldn't care less whether I caught that boat or not. Exhausted from my walk and feeling all the frustrations of my traveling style welling up inside me – the constant need to find a place to sleep, the watching every centavo, the loneliness of not encountering anyone I could speak to in English for weeks at a time - I blurted out "Think you could go any slower, pal? Try and finish before siesta time, eh." I was counting on this yokel not knowing English or, if he did, not being able to understand it at the speed I rattled off my insult.

The border agent paid me no mind, leisurely examining my visa and entry stamp. "I trust I'm not going to have to wait for you to learn how to sign your name," I spat out as he leafed languidly through the passport, looking for a blank page to stamp.

"*No te preocupe, senor*," he said calmly as he handed me back my passport, "*El barco va a esperar para ti.*" He was telling me not to worry, the ferry would wait for me.

Turning to go I saw that he was right. The ferry was still there, the smoke rising from its smokestacks indicating its readiness to depart but the crew lounging about nonchalantly in no apparent hurry to leave. I looked at my watch. It said 12:30.

Then it dawned on me. I was in Latin America, where they didn't let anything so inconsequential as a schedule impose constraints on their willingness to help out a fellow human being. If I had arrived an hour late, the ferry would probably still have been there waiting for me, the bus driver having informed the captain another passenger was on his way.

I felt ashamed. Here I was being totally obnoxious and the objects of my haughtiness were showing me special consideration. Many times in the past I had watched with contempt the antics of my fellow Americans, bellowing and fuming over some similarly frustrating circumstance, filled with their North American sense of urgency and their own self-importance. Now I realized I was no better.

"*Buen viaje*," the border agent shouted, waving goodbye from the doorway of his shed as I ran to board the boat.

"*Gracias*," I shouted back, humbled and apologetic. I wished I could stay and make amends

As the boat pulled away from the dock, a glimmer of sunlight burst through the dissipating cloud cover. The water of the lake glistened and reflected off the majestic, pine-clad mountains which hemmed it in. Overwhelmed by the beauty of it all, my relief at having made the boat, and the gratitude I felt toward those who had waited for me, I rejoiced within, "Oh beautiful, compassionate, backward Latin America, I love you!"

Chapter 8 – RIO DE JANEIRO

I made it to Rio de Janeiro the day before Carnival, just as Bill and Kathy and I had planned so many thousands of miles before. I wondered if they had made it, too. I had chatted with a lady at Iguazzu Falls a week earlier who, when she found out I was from Dallas, started telling me about this engaging couple from Dallas she'd met in La Paz, Bolivia. Bill and Kathy were so much out of my mind, she'd just about described them down to their underwear before I realized whom she was talking about. As I had predicted, they did ditch the car in Panama and were now hopping from city to city by plane. Traveling in that style they should have had no problem making it to Rio for Carnival, but I didn't encounter them at the usual Rio mail drops. I didn't know where else to look for them and was having too good a time to care. Years later I would learn they were in Rio at that time. I guess we didn't frequent the same nightspots (The trendy watering holes they frequented would not have been listed in Frommer's; mine neither, but for a different reason).

"Cidade maravilhosa" the Brazilians call Rio: The Marvelous City. And it is simply marvelous. The incredible beauty of the time-rounded gray, granitic peaks speckled with clumps of lush greenness, rising over crescents of creamy, white sand beaches; the smell of the ever-blooming, tropical flora accentuated by that of the street vendor's exotic juices and spicy *empanadas*; the sensuality which pervades everything, from the silent samba performed by the swaying

palms to the equally rhythmic, hip-swinging sashaying of the bikini-clad temptresses. It all worked to cause a metamorphosis in me. After all those years of toeing the line, of playing the career-driven game with an intensity which bordered on the psychotic, I succumbed to the allure of hedonism.

I found a room in Copacabana and a job teaching English at the *Insituto Brasil-Estados Unidos* (IBEU), an English-language center set up by the USIA. I spent most of my time on the beach, needing to dedicate only fifteen hours a week or so to my cushy, though not particularly remunerative, job. I worked on my body-surfing, on my tan, and on the tanned lovelies - foreign and domestic - who adorned the beach. In a word - or two, I became a beach bum.

Rio proved much more conducive to amorous pursuits than had the road to Rio. City girls were much more cosmopolitan, shall we say, than the small-town girls I had been limited to in my travels. There was the horny and willing Consuela - too plumb to pass my exacting standards normally, but to whom I granted a special waiver, as she possessed one endearing attribute, rare in the Brazilian girls I met: she owned a car. With her, I discovered, for the first time, the comical intricacies of trying to make love in the back seat of a Volkswagen. I had missed out on automobile-based romance when I was in high school, not being that cool; now I was learning how to wedge legs, arms, torsos in a contorted, motorized mating ritual. But it all came to an abrupt end one night when Consuela and I, parked on a remote beach, contorted ourselves into position when a light shined through the window announced that the police had arrived. We unscrewed ourselves (literally and figuratively) and hastily put on some clothes. Her panicked, tearful pleading with the policemen not to expose her wicked ways to her family would have torn at my heartstrings, had I cared anything about her. As it was, I observed the spectacle nonchalantly, hurling an occasional snide remark about the "amigos do Papa" at the police, knowing my American passport protected me from a pistol whipping.

Then there was Maria Helena. Half black, half Amazon Indian, she was the beautiful consort of a New Yorker I met who was down from the States on vacation. About twenty years old and obviously from a background of poverty, she appeared to have no family in the area. She spoke vaguely of brothers and sisters somewhere up north, but, as best I could tell, she was on her own - a woman of the streets. She had not succumbed to assuming that role professionally as yet, however, and restricted the bestowing of her favors to those she chose, though with the expectation her generosity would be rewarded almost as contractually had an amount been expressly agreed upon.

One night she and I were lounging on the couch in her benefactor's apartment, listening to the melodious sounds of Chico Buarque de Hollanda and drinking *cachaça*, the sugar cane-based liquor Brazilians favor. I considered her a kept woman, but her keeper had gone to bed in the other room. Emboldened by the romantic strains of Chico's guitar, the balmy night air, warm as a caress, and several rounds of *cachaça*, I started to stroke her soft, velveteen hair. She turned toward me with a smile as sweet as the Mona Lisa, though considerably less enigmatic. As she pressed her full, dark lips against my own, I slipped my hand under her cheap, cotton blouse and fondled her full, upright breasts. Anxious lest her benefactor should waken from his inebriated slumber, she suggested we go to my place a few blocks away. Apparently, it was not unusual for her to spend the night away.

We walked down side streets, avoiding the main drag, *Avenida Atlantico*, bustling even at this late hour. I feared running into some acquaintance from the higher social stratum I sought to foster relationships in, knowing they would not approve of my companion or the act I was so obviously about to engage in with her. I don't know if Maria Helena feared an encounter of a similar, though inverted, kind, but she seemed to prefer the back route, too. Our eager anticipation of what lay in store at the end of our stroll was palpable.

We spent a passionate night together and repeated the tryst several times in the weeks that followed. Initially, I considered Maria Helena nothing more than a one-night stand, so I was surprised to find myself feeling genuine affection for her over time. Despite her manifest familiarity with carnal pleasures, she still retained that air of sweet innocence I found so alluring in her less experienced compatriots. She seemed fond of me, too. In fact, she showed worrisome signs of being emotionally dependent on the relationship. She didn't seem to mind that I was contributing nothing to her financial well-being, that aspect of her life continuing to be taken care of by the New Yorker.

Eventually, I came to consider Maria Helena a liability, the novelty of the thing having worn off, and the disparity in our backgrounds outweighing my horny regard. I started making excuses why we couldn't get together. Looking up at me with those big, doe-like, innocent eyes, I knew she didn't know why I was acting the way I was. Touched but unrelenting, I continued to put her off. Then, when she telephoned my school trying to reach me and had a little too revealing a conversation with my boss, I broke off the relationship entirely.

I didn't see Maria Helena again until several months later, shortly before I left Brazil. I was strolling down the wavy-tiled sidewalk that runs along Copacabana beach one evening when an overly made up, overly friendly young lady, obviously a prostitute, approached me and asked if I desired some quick sexual gratification. Without waiting for an answer she began tugging me towards the beach, where I could see several of her colleagues plying their trade out amongst the candlelit offerings to *Pele*, the Goddess of the Sea, left by practitioners of that peculiarly Brazilian, Catholico-pagan religion, *Candomble*. As she dragged me cajolingly along, we passed under a street light which illuminated our faces. We recognized each other simultaneously. It was a much older looking, much more savvy, much degraded Maria Helena I saw. We stood there facing each other in silence. I felt guilty and embarrassed; she looked plaintive but resigned. There was nothing to be said. I walked away.

I think of Maria Helena sometimes and wonder about my attitude towards her. She was a better person than many of the higher class girls I treated with more respect. Even when I had feelings for her, I saw her as little more than a tramp. I try to convince myself that I saw her this way because she was a tramp, not because of the color of her skin or her impoverished origins, but who knows? I wish I had treated her better. I hope someone else did.

Beside the post-coital remorse aroused by Maria Helena, one other unpleasantness intruded upon the reverie of my rakish existence. I'd gone to the American Embassy to pick up my mail upon arriving in Rio and amongst the letters was one from my draft board ordering me to report for a physical examination, the first step in the process of being drafted. The date on which I was supposed to appear was a month previous. I estimated I was somewhere in the highlands of Bolivia on that date, *incommunicado* and working on being *in flagrante delicto* - in the sexual, not criminal, sense.

Had the date of my physical been a week or two in the future, I might have just ended my grand tour and flown home. But since I had already missed it by a month, what would be the difference if I missed it by two or even three months? Rio was just too enticing to leave so soon after arriving. Sitting there in the park across the street from the American Embassy, the draft board's letter clutched in my hand, gazing out over the placid waters of Guanabara Bay towards its massive, loaf-shaped gatekeeper, I decided to look for a room and a job instead of a plane ticket. It was a fateful decision.

I adopted delaying tactics with the draft board. I fired off a very polite letter, explaining why I had not appeared as ordered, inquiring whether I could take the physical examination in Brazil, and requesting a 2-A occupational deferment as a teacher. The board responded that the only place I could take the exam outside the United States was the Canal Zone and that my request for a deferment had been denied as teachers were no longer deferred. I wrote back and told them I was committed to my teaching position until June and would return then. They didn't wait to find out if I meant it. In May they declared me delinquent and told me they were putting me at the top of the list for induction. In June they issued the induction notice ordering me to report for duty in July. As with the notice for the physical, I didn't receive the letter containing this order until after the date on which I was supposed to report.

I really wanted to take the physical exam. There was the off chance I might garner that most coveted of Selective Service classifications: 4-F, physically unfit. A friend had gotten one, thanks to a sympathetic examining doctor and an old football injury to his knee that didn't keep him from playing soccer throughout college.

Another friend, anxious to serve in the Air Force but when that fell through deciding to skip the military thing altogether, jacked up his blood sugar level by consuming mounds of candy bars the night before the exam so that he appeared to be diabetic. Then there was my traveling companion, Bill. He had parlayed a week in the mental health clinic in college into a 4-F for mental instability, the army requiring you be sane to participate in the insanity going on in Southeast Asia. I'd even heard of someone who was turned down for bad acne. I couldn't think of anything that might disqualify me, but you never know. I didn't think I'd try the ruse of showing up for the physical in a dress and kiss the doctor. Actually, I heard about that one in San Francisco, so maybe it wasn't a ruse.

I had some serious thinking to do. I remembered back to the night of our departure from Dallas when Bill's dad had taken me aside and told me confidentially that, if I had any problems with the draft, to let him know. He was a nice man, a veteran of World War II, who had always treated me like an adopted son (My own father died when I was young). I was grateful for his kind concern but shocked at the suggestion that "things can be arranged." I didn't want to believe the system worked that way; and, in fact, I didn't believe it. I suspected at the time he made the offer I would never take him up on it, and now that the moment of decision had arrived I still didn't like it. Whether it was because I found it sleazy or because I didn't want to be indebted to him, I can't say.

In some ways, ending my odyssey and going home was the easiest option. I assumed that, despite my tardiness, all would be forgiven if I just showed up and allowed myself to be drafted into the army. I'll admit that this appeared to be the most honorable course of action at the time, as well. But I hated to terminate my traveling. I was really enjoying myself and felt I was learning things as important as what I had learned in college. Not the stuff I was learning about women, though that was something I didn't learn about in college either, but about other cultures, world history, international economics, things like that. My horizon had been enormously broadened - just what travel is supposed to do. I wondered if I would have the opportunity to pick up where I left off after my two years of military service. Life seems so short when you're young.

If I could show up a month late for my induction without any adverse consequences, I speculated, maybe I could show up six months late or even a year. By then perhaps I would have seen all the things I wanted to see and be ready to go home and do my duty. Choosing this option was especially appealing because it didn't require any resolute decision on my part; I could just continue doing what I was doing. So that's what I did.

Months of agonized soul-searching followed. I had never broken the law before, if that was in fact what I had now done. I was concerned about what my family, my friends, the society at large would think of me, as failing to do my duty was not what they had come to expect from me. I fretted over what might be the consequences for my career prospects. I castigated myself for being engaged in the frivolous pursuit of women while my peers were risking their lives in the jungles of Vietnam. At the same time I tried to figure out what the war was all about. What I learned, as well as my personal exposure to American foreign policy in my travels through Latin America, was less than inspiring. My mind was a maelstrom of confused and contending thoughts, abstract and concrete, practical and romantic, selfless and self-interested, courageous and cowardly. Many a time I woke up from a nightmare in the middle of the night to find myself lying on the floor in a cold sweat.

As far as my family went, they never put any pressure on me to return or expressed a critical remark. I did get a somewhat frantic letter from my sister, Martha, saying the FBI had called and told her, if I came home right away and reported for induction, all would be forgiven. But there was no suggestion from her as to how I should respond, which for a sweetly meddling busybody like Martha must have been especially hard to omit. This was in September of 1968, three months after I'd been ordered to report for induction. I was pleased to see my assumption about being able to delay the day of judgment a while was proving true... so far.

My friends, in general, were more politically aware than I was, or at least than I was before I left the States. But most of them had found one way or the other to finagle out of the draft and so didn't have strong feelings about Vietnam or draft-dodging, as far as I knew. They were, for the most part, engaged in that frenetic, career-establishing stage of their lives, which left them little time for anything else. They just weren't personally involved in the Vietnam thing and probably looked upon those of us who were as objects of curiosity more than as recipients of condemnation or commendation. As to the peers who were doing the fighting, any guilt I felt for not joining them was muted by the fact that I couldn't think of anyone I knew who had actually been drafted, much less sent to Vietnam, such rarefied air did I socialize in. I felt sorry for the men fighting and dying, but I figured we had all faced the same choice - to go or not to go - and now we all had to face the consequences of our decision.

This rationalization satisfied me with regard to those I assumed had let themselves be drafted out of fear of the law, a lack of imagination as to what other options they might have, or a lack of initiative in pursuing those options. It didn't work so well with regard to those I assumed truly thought it was their duty to go and had responded bravely. But with the country divided over where the moral high ground lay, I didn't have much trouble convincing myself that where the call of duty beckoned was not clear. The celebrity draft resister I had met at Stanford, David Harris, was then facing imprisonment for his beliefs. That seemed pretty brave to me, too.

As to society at large, it was become increasingly fractured over the war and the draft. My own college, Dartmouth, which had been a haven of apathy towards anything that didn't involve sports or women when I was there, was now experiencing occasional campus turmoil over the draft. If I wanted any moral underpinning for my "refusal" to be drafted, there were now many people willing to provide it. I was starting to read some of the critics of our motives and methods in Vietnam and finding them more and more convincing. Still, if I continued on my present course, I knew it would not stand me in good stead with most of my fellow countrymen whenever I returned home. This consideration was still important to me back then.

I tried to estimate what the effect of my present course of action on my future career might be. Despite having stepped off the career track by dropping out of the Stanford Business School, I still had big plans for myself. I wasn't sure what those plans were, but I saw myself achieving success, as conventionally defined, in some form. But this particular item on my resume wasn't going to help much in that regard. The question was how much was it going to hurt. I found myself heretically speculating, "Should I care?"

If my conception of duty led me to refuse to be drafted, I should be willing to sacrifice my career for that "cause". Others who had a different conception of duty were risking much more, after all. My reading and thinking on Vietnam had progressed to the point where I considered it possible my duty as a decent, peace-loving human being called on me to counter the war effort, not join it. But I still had a problem with this course of action from a logical perspective. I'm not a pacifist, so I accept that countries can call on their citizens to take up arms in self-defense. If the duly-elected authorities decide a war must be fought, it's up to the citizenry to respond dutifully. The citizens can't very well be allowed to pick and choose which armed conflicts they consider "just" and which not. Logically, the only way you could justify not doing your duty is if you believed the system of government which issued the call was illegitimate. I wasn't ready to subscribe to that belief and so had trouble justifying my course of action logically.

I've never been bothered by those who attribute my decision to dodge the draft to a lack of courage. I really don't think courage ever entered the picture. I knew I could die over there, but I don't think I was ever able to truly project myself into the stark terror of a combat situation. Courage might be attributed to those who can foresee what they are getting into and still press on, but I'm not one of those. Those times when I have acted in a way some might consider brave have been times when my lack of foresight got me into tight situations. I had to act in an apparently brave manner in order to extricate myself from my own stupidity. Like the time I plunged into humongous storm surf off Copacabana to do some body-surfing and had to be rescued by Brazilians half my size. Had I gone to Vietnam, I would have left the States with the same sense of my own invincibility I think most of those who went felt. It doesn't take much courage to board a troop ship when you are convinced you're invincible and cannot foresee what lies ahead.

No, for me, the question of the draft was a question of duty, not personal courage. So if you want to criticize me for evading the draft, criticize me for not doing my duty, not for being a coward. But, if you do criticize me, be ready to prove down which road the path of duty lay. If, on the other hand, you praise me for refusing to serve, be ready to prove I didn't just mold my conception of duty to fit the path that was most convenient for me to tread.

And so, with thoughts like these ricocheting around in my head, I meandered into draft evasion. To continue down the road I had started on was the easiest path, so that's the one I took. "*Carpe diem*", as the hippies said. Tomorrow would take care of itself. Little did I suspect how many tomorrows would creep in my peripatetic pace from day to day until the last syllable uttered by a federal judge.

Chapter 9 – MARIE INES

"I'm a communist," the young lady in combat fatigues announced as she stepped by me into the classroom.

"Nice to meet you. I'm a Gemini," I responded.

The young lady was Marie Ines, the student I would get to know best of all my students (know in the personal, not biblical, sense). I don't know whether she introduced herself that way to get a rise out of me or just to let me know where she stood. She succeeded in doing both. Marie Ines would get many rises out of me in the weeks to come (again, emotional, not physical).

She was nineteen, a university student, who lived with her parents in a comfortable apartment in Copacabana. She was attractive enough but not a beauty. She always dressed "*a moda da revolucion*": combat boots, a T-shirt emblazoned with the intense gaze of Che Guevara, a tattered army jacket, a black beret. She was enrolled in my highest level course, "American History and Literature," so her English was very good.

Marie Ines belonged to the "radical student element", as *Newsweek* might call it in reporting on the political situation in Brazil. With an unpopular military regime in power, it was not clear whether she and her friends represented a radical element or the mainstream. She introduced me to Marx, Trotsky, Franz Fanon, Regis Debray - authors I'd never read, or in some cases even heard of - who expressed views I'd never been exposed to. When she knew me well enough to know I'd not be offended, she delighted in calling me "the class enemy."

She also was the one who told me about the student restaurant not far from where I worked in downtown Rio. Its prices appealed to my proletarian budget, so I decided to try it. It took a student card to get in, so with an innocent, confused look, many "*não compreendo*"'s, and a sheepish grin, I bamboozled the front office into accepting my expired college ID as a valid ticket of entry. I purchased a bowl of the Brazilian national dish, *feijoada*, which is sort of like a bland chili only with pig entrails instead of real meat, and took a seat in the enormous dining hall.

Up in the front of the hall a Fidel Castro-wannabe was standing on a table haranguing a crowd of animated, placard-toting students. Their signs read "*Abaixó ditadura! Abaixó imperialismo!*," which even I understood called for taking down the dictatorship and imperialism. I was jotting all this down on mental index cards like a good student of social dynamics, which is what I considered myself, when one of the students gathered round the speaker noticed me sitting in the back of the room. In no time I was surrounded by a vociferous, gesticulating mob of angry students. I was shocked at their hostility; they really didn't like me – me, mild, easygoing, friend to the world Ken!

"But they don't even know me!" I protested silently to myself. I knew it was my country of origin (made plain by the Dallas Cowboys t-shirt I was wearing), not any personal dislike, which provoked their ire (Note to self: get t-shirt with red maple leaf; sprinkle your conversation with "eh"s.). Spittle-laden epithets, some of which I recognized as unkind at best, were being hurled at me. I didn't know whether to play possum, i.e., assume a meek and humble demeanor, or fight back like a cornered cougar, i.e., let fly with the same sort of taunts and insults as those directed at me. I was emboldened by the fact I stood a half-foot taller than most of them, but their numerical advantage was disconcerting. Reasoning that a torrent of foulmouthed English would be lost on them anyway, I opted for the aggrieved innocent stratagem.

It was starting to get ugly. Someone was about to toss some hot tea in my face, when Marie Ines emerged from the throng and, placing her body as a barrier between them and me, addressed them in rapid-fire Portuguese. Here's what she had to say as best as I could understand it.

"*Companheiros!* This gringo is not a spy! I know him. He's just a stupid, ignorant *norte-americano* looking for a cheap bowl of *feijoada*. He means us no harm; in fact, he sympathizes with our cause. We must learn to distinguish between Americans like him and those who are true agents of imperialism. Americans like this can become our allies if we educate them properly. Look at all the Americans refusing to fight in Vietnam. They're sick of imperialism, too. *O povo unido jamais será vencido!*" ("The people, united, will never be defeated!")

At the sound of that evocative rallying cry I had heard time and again across Latin America, the crowd burst into a cheer. Marie Ines had won the day. The anger on the students faces melted away, just as they melted away to rejoin the cadres being harangued by the bearded Cicero atop the lunch table.

"You'll have to forgive them," Marie Ines said turning to me, "We're demonstrating today and they're a little stirred up." With that, she scampered off to join her comrades.

I couldn't believe my good luck in her appearing when she did and was thankful she knew me as well as she did. She knew I didn't scoff at her revolutionary fervor and that I had read many of the books she'd lent me. She'd taken me along on some of her field trips to the *favelas* (slums) so I could see firsthand what the revolution was all about. She knew of my situation vis-à-vis the draft. She wasn't a knight but a lady and her armor wasn't shining but faded, but she was Sir Galahad to me.

Later that day, from the vantage point of my eighth-floor classroom, I watched the soldiers, backed by tanks, clearing the students from the streets with tear gas and occasional shots. The terrified, fleeing students presented quite a different picture than the stoked-up accusers who had confronted me in the restaurant. I reflected on how easy it was to engage in revolutionary rhetoric, how much more difficult to maintain your dedication to the cause when confronted by a tank.

I wondered about the depth of Marie Ines's conviction. Was she really dedicated to the revolution or just being trendy? Her social roots were not with the downtrodden masses, but then neither were those of many revolutionary leaders – Lenin, Castro, our own George Washington. I knew she was a caring person, but it would take more than that to see her through the arrest, imprisonment, torture that might lie ahead. The hard-line reaction of the military government to the students' peaceful demonstration suggested she would be given ample opportunity to prove her dedication to the cause in the days to come.

Chapter 10 – EXPATS

Though I greatly enjoyed the Brazilians I knew, I spent most of my time in Rio within the familiar confines of the American community - *"Os gringos"* to the Brazilians. I found my fellow expatriates a curious breed. In most cases, American "expats" do not differ much from their French, British, Canadian, or German counterparts in the adjustments - mental and moral - they make to the circumstance of living outside their native land. The one thing distinctive about American expatriate communities is the regrettable proportion of its members who make no accommodation to the local culture, other than to adopt an even more narrow-minded, chauvinistic, condescending attitude than they had when they arrived. They would take every opportunity to bemoan their fate, complaining about everything from the unreliable phone service to the tropical heat. These cocooned xenophobes gained no insight into the people amongst whom they were living no matter how long they resided "in-country". The locals forever remained for them little yellow/brown/black savages with lazy habits, body odor, an indigestible cuisine, and incomprehensible English. But let's not dwell on these poor, shriveled up souls. Let me introduce you to a couple of Americans I knew in Rio of a different ilk.

Bob was Director of Classes at the *Instituto-Brasil Estados Unidos*. He was a chubby, middle-aged American who had been born and raised in Brazil, his father being the manager of the local branch of an American conglomerate. He was a pleasant fellow with an easygoing manner and a quick wit. His mannerisms made me suspect he was a homosexual, a conclusion one did not jump to quickly in those closet-filled days (Back then people thought Liberace was just being theatrical, as one wit put it). When my Copacabana landlady kicked me out for my dalliance with Maria Helena, Bob invited me to move in with him in his house in Ipanema. His Brazilian house mate, a svelte young man, made room for me by moving out of his room into Bob's. When I saw there was only one bed in Bob's room, I felt my suspicions had been confirmed.

Bob's attitude towards the war and my position with the draft was, as far as I could tell, one of total disinterest. He couldn't seem to care less whether I saluted the flag or spat on it. Growing up abroad, he'd escaped the insular perspective we homegrown types are prone to. Having missed out on all the rah-rah stuff – the Fourth of July parades, John Wayne movies, pledging allegiance at every public gathering - from little league games to Alcoholics Anonymous meetings – he cast a jaundiced eye on expressions of America's loftier aims abroad, just like his Brazilian neighbors. He was neither proud nor ashamed to be an American; he just was one.

Bob could afford to adopt a nonchalant attitude towards patriotism because he had never been subject to the draft. There was some special classification sons of Americans living abroad fit into and it meant they usually did not have to serve. If Bob ever was subject to the draft, his sexual orientation provided an easy out.

Bob treated the saga of my ongoing skirmishes with my draft board as a joke. "Heard anything from your friends back home lately?" he would ask casually from time to time, the hint of a grin on his face. With me feeling like the whole country stood united in condemnation of what I was doing, that was enough to qualify him as a friend.

Bob would take me up to his family's vacation home in the mountains behind Rio on the weekend. There I got many insights into the lifestyle of an American - rich by local standards, moderately well-to-do in his countrymen's eyes - living in an underdeveloped country. Any belief in the dignity of human labor which might have led one to mow his lawn or fix his car himself back home was subverted by the irresistible cheapness of letting other humans do the dirty work down here. You belonged to the best clubs, where the pool or tennis courts might be inferior to public facilities back home but were the best in town – *tout en haut.* You hobnobbed with the *crème de la crème* of local society. Even I - an indigent, itinerant nobody - gained entrée into social circles I would have been shunned from back home, simply because of the way I looked, the passport I carried, and the accent-less English I spoke. All in all, it was a heady experience, sure to feed one's inbred sense of American superiority.

Steve started teaching at the IBEU a few months after I did. He was an unassuming, soft-spoken guy a couple of years older than I, an ex-Navy Seal fresh from Vietnam. He didn't know my draft status and I had never heard of the Seals, so we got along fine. Even after we got to know each other and each other's position with regard to the war, he refrained from calling me a coward and I refrained from asking him about killing babies.

Steve's attitude towards his service in Vietnam puzzled me. He showed neither braggadocio nor remorse. He seemed to look on it simply as a job he did that he didn't do anymore, and now he just wanted to get on with his life. He was intent on exploring for diamonds in some of the remoter parts of the Amazon River basin. His stories of slashing through dense tropical undergrowth to set up camp, scuba diving in murky 100-foot deep sink holes to retrieve the diamonds, and carrying a rifle to bed in case of a tiger attack made me think he had just the right training for the job. He invited me to join him, but I didn't think my business school training would stand me in as good stead.

I, on the other hand, was appalled by some of the things he told me about his time as a Seal. He described one course requirement at the Seals' training school in Little Creek, Virginia. The trainees were required to catch one of the stray cats roaming the base and chew off its head in front of their classmates. Steve thought this barbaric ritual perfectly normal, the sort of toughening up men had to undergo in order to be dependable in the kill-or-be-killed conditions of war. He may be right, but I wondered who deprogrammed these deranged killers before they were released back into polite society after their service was up. Steve seemed to have escaped with his humanity intact, but then many serial killers appear normal to family and friends until their alter ego is exposed.

Steve told me of one operation where his platoon had been detailed to sneak into a village in the dead of night and kill a young man who was suspected of collaborating with the Vietcong. This was under Operation Phoenix, a CIA brainchild, born of frustration with the tendency of the local court system not to prosecute those who hadn't broken the law. So, the CIA used the Seals to simply do away with suspected collaborators in accordance with their own conception of due process. The program made the worst vigilantes of the Old West look like model citizens.

Steve and his mates got their man, but in withdrawing from the village they could hear the aroused villagers chasing after them. The Seals lay down in the tall grass; then, when the villagers came within range, fired at random. Steve told me about it as matter of factly as if he were describing a play in a football game. I, on the other hand, envisioned dozens of unarmed villagers – men, women, children – gunned down as they tried to apprehend the murderers of one of their own. No wonder we lost.

One of Steve's more bizarre theories about war was that the wounds you carried away from the battlefield, so long as you weren't carried off yourself, were no big deal.

"So you lose a leg and walk with a limp," he would argue, "It adds character, like Long John Silver."

His own body bore the scars of several character-building episodes, so I guess he should know, but I found it unconvincing. Maybe he was trying to minimize the downside to military service, thinking fear was what motivated my reluctance to join in the slaughter. Sometimes, in retrospect, I wonder if Steve was as "ex" as he made out. Was he still in government service, officially or voluntarily, and been assigned me as part of his case load? It seems unlikely the wheels of government could spin that quickly, or that the massive war machine would waste any effort on one insignificant draft dodger, but who knows? In any case, at the time it never occurred to me to question Steve's sincerity. Nor did it occur to me to link him with rumors I'd heard about American Special Forces being engaged in covert counter-insurgency efforts in the wilds of the Amazon. Who's ever heard of diamonds in Brazil, anyway?

When I began my second semester teaching at the IBEU, I found I had been assigned fewer courses than I had the previous semester, which worried me as it meant less income. Bob claimed it was because fewer students than expected had signed up and he was trying to distribute the workload instead of letting teachers go. I had noticed that Bob's attitude toward me had become somewhat reserved in recent weeks. I wondered whether his limiting my course load wasn't a strategic move in that the paramount geopolitical issue of the day: getting Ken back home to be inducted. The IBEU was affiliated in some way with the United States Information Agency (USIA). So, it's not hard for me to imagine that when my case was turned over to the FBI in July of 1968, they notified the folks at the American embassy in Rio, who took it upon themselves to see what they could do to get me home. One thing they could do was deny me my livelihood since Bob was in no position to refuse them, no matter what personal empathy he might have felt for me.

It may sound farfetched to those of you who have never had occasion to have the mammoth, super-secret, national security apparatus take an interest in you, and it sounds a little far-fetched to me even now, but who knows? The beauty of this is-anybody-behind-the-curtain? game is that everyone can believe himself right, since, except in rare cases, nobody outside the barbed wire-topped walls of our secret agencies is ever going to know what really happened. The game is, of course, less fun when it's *your* life that's being manipulated.

Whatever the case may have been, the upshot was that I decided to leave Rio. But not, as my "handlers" hoped, for home. I decided I would circumnavigate, or more precisely, circumambulate the globe. I estimated it would take me a year or two. Surely by then the war in Vietnam would be over, which might facilitate the resolution of this little unpleasantry with the draft in a manner mutually satisfactory to me and the legal system without even greater unpleasantness coming into play. (What's that they say about an optimist, he just hasn't had enough experience?

Chapter 11 – NORTH AFRICA

In October 1968, after eight months in Rio and almost a year into my odyssey, I boarded an inelegant but seaworthy Portuguese liner bound for Barcelona, Spain. My next destination, as much as I had one, was Israel. I had met an Israeli teenager in Rio, Doreen - a hot, sassy sabra who had raved about her homeland. I thought I had about enough money to get that far before it ran out, and Israel seemed like a good place to stop and earn some more.

As I had already done Europe, I chose to traverse the Mediterranean by the southern route - across North Africa. I first set foot in the Arab world in Morocco, where I debarked after crossing the Strait of Gibraltar from Spain. Even coming from as Moorish-influenced a country as Spain, the cultural differences between Morocco and any country I had ever been in was startling. Preconceptions about the Arabs formed from Hollywood movies and historical narratives laden with religious animosity dating back to the Crusades engendered fear and mistrust. Under every *djellaba* (hooded cloak), I envisioned a curved dagger, clutched and at the ready. Behind every favor, unctuously extended, I looked for a trick.

At first, my preconceptions stood me in good stead. My first night was spent in a little town called Larache, fifty or so miles south of Tangiers. Two Canadian girls equally leery of the villainous Arabs had latched onto me as security. Since one of them was quite attractive, I was happy to let myself be latched onto; I was hoping to do a little latching myself later that evening. The girls, with me in tow, were befriended by a lanky, affable Moroccan, complete with fez and pointed slippers straight out of a Hollywood wardrobe department. Omar - or whatever his name was - invited us to the local tea house, that being the beverage of choice in this Muslim country. I was struck upon entering the brightly-lit establishment to see there wasn't a woman in the place, just cloaked, mustachioed men, smoking water pipes, playing backgammon, and staring at us as they would at animals in the zoo. It must have been really creepy for the girls; though, blissfully unaware of what was going on around me as usual, that thought didn't enter my mind at the time.

Omar dazzled us with promises of things to come – a couscous dinner, a place to sleep, a camel ride in the morning – as we downed mint tea served in petite glasses. When the bill came, the girls and I let it sit there. After all, Omar had invited us. After studiously ignoring the bill for several minutes, Omar finally blurted out "You owe 25 francs." We were not only paying for our own drinks but Omar's as well. Who was the host and who the guests had been magically reversed – Abracadabra! So much for the famous Arab hospitality to strangers.

Still, we considered it a good investment in cordiality in light of all the nice things Omar was going to do for us (Being new to the country, we didn't realize the price of tea had been jacked up to three times the going rate for the esteemed visitors!). Omar led us to an apartment where we were to have our couscous dinner. Seated in the bare living room were five or six Arab men - our hosts, Omar told us. After introducing us to his friends, Omar suggested he and I go off to see about those camel rides for the morrow. Oblivious to what was going on, I said "OK" and got up to go. The girls grabbed my arm, and taking me aside, demanded I not leave them there alone. So, I gave Omar some excuse why I couldn't join him and he left alone.

Our "hosts" didn't look or act like hosts. They spoke neither English nor French, or so we surmised from our attempts to engage them in conversation in languages we knew. They just sat there, saying nothing, except to whisper to each other in Arabic every so often. After our attempts at friendly chitchat had been met with sullen stares and nervous fidgeting, we gave up and just stared back.

The atmosphere was eerily tense. It was beginning to dawn on me what was going on. I didn't smell any couscous cooking in the kitchen. In fact, glancing that way, I didn't see anything in the kitchen to cook or anything to cook with! The apartment was obviously not lived in.

After a few minutes of this awkward stand-off, Omar returned and, after some gibberish in Arabic with his friends, abruptly announced the dinner was off. We bade a curt goodbye to our hosts, which was returned in silence, and Omar took us to a run-down hotel done in tattered French colonial where the seedy innkeeper assured us we were getting "the best room in the place". It was a dump, with two sagging beds, a bare overhead light, and no hot water. But in one respect it was the best room in the hotel: the price he charged us for it the next morning.

Even now, after much experience with Arabs, I'm still not sure what took place, or almost took place, in that apartment. Would the girls have suffered some unwanted advances from the men - to put it mildly - had I left with Omar? I don't know. I can believe all the men wanted was to gaze upon some females who weren't hidden behind veils (Moroccan women do the full reverse monty with only heavily made up eyes visible). I can imagine it could have been much worse, something that might make the papers back in Canada. I didn't know it at the time but from Arab men's perspective, accustomed to the restrictive rules governing their own women's behavior, two women traveling as the Canadians were, especially in the company of a man, were nothing but wanton harlots, ready for and deserving of anything.

I split up with the Canadians the next day. They sprinted down the road to Marrakesh, a relatively safe haven as it was a Mecca for Western hippies, while I headed east towards Algeria. I can't remember meeting any other Western girls at all in my trip across North Africa. I suppose they just couldn't take the Arab men, who made the whistling, gesturing, butt-pinching Italians look like models of decorum. A story making the rounds in the low budget travel circuit about two vagabondesses who had been gang-raped in accommodations they had been offered for the night did nothing to promote female tourism, especially as the accommodations were in the local police station, and the rapists, the police! I think the story was apocryphal, but it was believable enough to scare my Canadian friends and probably many others.

The Arab males' attitude toward women not only thwarted the travel plans of peripatetic Western women but me, too. The seclusion of women meant I was seldom invited into an Arab's house, for it was there that the women went unveiled. So I spent many a night sleeping in some damp, chilly field, being woken from a fitful sleep by the pre-dawn call to prayer from some nearby mosque. The honor-bound status of women stymied baser desires than just my desire for a good night's sleep. It meant local girls were off limits (Oh, for the good old days with those wanton Catholic village girls of Latin America!). The importance placed on virgin brides meant any premature defoliation might be a matter of life and death for the defoliator as well as the defoliatee. Common opinion amongst westerners was that, if an Arab man avenged himself on a daughter or sister for bringing shame upon the family, including in his revenge, perhaps, the foolhardy stud, he stood a good chance of being let off scot-free.

The penalties of messing with Arab women didn't really affect my love life, as there was little to pique my interest – just shapeless, Klan-like ghosts, whatever beauty lying beneath effectively concealed. You would think not being exposed constantly to views of female flesh would free my mind from too much concentration on sex to engage in loftier thoughts, and it did to a degree. Being surrounded by Muslim women - lumpy, moving, bundles of cloth – suggested a basic contradiction in the clothing style of liberated Western women. They decry being treated as sex objects, yet dress as if they want to be. I'm not talking about the blatant, mini-skirted, cleavage-showing provocateurs. Even a buttoned up business suit reveals enough of a woman's physiognomy to arouse the male libido. So, you western women who are put off by the leering, unwanted advances of your men, here's a suggestion: dress like Muslim women. Even that might not work, however. It's amazing how much sensuality can be conveyed by just the eyes! The occasional provocative look from unveiled eyes worked on my libido like the latest issue of *Playboy*.

So I wended my way along the coast from Morocco to Egypt, only occasionally distracted by shapely legs or rounded breasts as I partook of the culture and history of the austral shore of the Mediterranean. I was amazed by what I discovered: the walled city of Fez, much more evocative of medieval times than Carcassone, its European equivalent in southern France; Leptis Magna in Libya, the most impressive roman ruins I've ever seen (and I've seen a few!), and, of course, the pyramids, the flat-topped one of which I had the opportunity to climb. I'd never heard of many of these places or knew much about the history of the people who built and/or lived in them. Before I passed through the former stomping grounds of the Barbary pirates, I didn't know where the "Tripoli" commemorated in the Marines' Hymn was. I'd heard of the Phoenicians – they gave us our alphabet after all – but wasn't prepared for the revelation that hit me while viewing the ruins of Carthage, the loser in repeated wars with Rome: but for the Alpine cold, we might now be trekking to Tunisia, instead of Italy, to visit the ruins of our cultural forefathers.

My exposure to the customs and lifestyle of the North Africans led me to conclude that all those whose coasts were lapped by the Mediterranean, i.e. those on both the African and European side of the sea, had more in common with each other than they did with the others who cohabited their respective continents. The siesta-inducing, al fresco eating rituals; the loud, gesticulating conversational style; the sanctity of the home and family; the centrality of the Church or the Mosque in daily life; the special status of women - idolized and therefore sequestered - characterized Spanish, Greek, Italian culture almost as much as it did the Arab. It seemed the Alps denoted more than just a physical barrier dividing the Middle-of-the-Earth-oriented southern Europeans from their Asian steppe-descended fellow Europeans to the north. Only a common religion united them, just as the lack of one divided them from the Muslims on the opposite shore.

One trait in which the Arabs resembled their fellow Mediterraneans was in their gracious and generous manners. From the Egyptian bureaucrat who never failed to offer me one of his Marlboros whenever he lit up, until the pittance he received in salary and the high price of imported cigarettes dawned on me and I declined further offers, to the half-starved-looking Libyan bedouins who shared their meager repast of a near meatless camel knee stew with me, I was always welcomed in the countries I passed through with unfailing hospitality (Omar, the mendacious Moroccan, notwithstanding). In light of this kindness, I felt bad about finding funny the remark some American had written in the autograph book a teenage Egyptian proudly showed me to prove how "many, many 'merykan friends" he had. Reflecting the epidemic-level, eye disease in Egypt which causes too many Egyptians to have a clouded-over eye or two and perhaps frustrated at being cheated once too often in the *souk* (bazaar), the "friend" had written: "If you ever meet an Arab with two good eyes, trust him. He's not an Arab." When Mohamed, or whoever, asked me what it said, I lied "He hopes to see you in America someday."

What made the Arabs' attitude toward me, an American, especially remarkable was the fact that it had only been a little over a year since what we and the Israelis call "The Six Day War". Many Arabs held the United States as much as Israel guilty for their defeat. Yet, despite the howling accusations levelled against the United States in the Arab media, the Arab man-in-the-street distinguished between individual citizens of a country and the policies of their government, a distinction too many Americans fail to make under similar circumstances. I contrasted my experience in the Arab world with that of German-Americans during World War I and Japanese-Americans during World War II. We couldn't even make the distinction with regard to our own fellow citizens!

Ironically, or maybe not so ironically, those Arabs who were hostile to me tended to be the better educated ones, as if being able to read and, hence, be manipulated by those who wrote was a prerequisite for instilling a blind hatred. In less literate, less connected societies it's not so easy to foment hate through ugly caricature (think apelike Japs), bogus atrocity stories (think Belgian babies impaled on German bayonets), and baseless fears (think Cold War-era missile gap). The Arabs, I suspect, cannot hope to defeat Israel until they have attained the level of "civilization" where an all-pervasive, drum-pounding, rabble-rousing mass media can turn their countries into very uncomfortable places for someone like me at times of national crisis.

The 1967 Arab-Israeli war changed the course of politics in the Middle East. Of somewhat less global significance, it also resulted in a momentous redirection in my personal life. When I reached Egypt I learned that you could no longer hitchhike from Cairo to Tel Aviv (Actually, you couldn't before the war either, but let's not muddy the picture). The erstwhile border between Egypt and Israel had moved westward to the Suez Canal, and it was delineated by barbed wire, big guns, and heavily armed men on both sides. To reach Israel I would have to take a boat to Cyprus, then another boat from Cyprus to Israel. Each leg of the trip cost about $25. I only had about $25. For the same fare I could take a boat to Beirut. I had met some travelers who had just come from Beirut and raved about "The Paris of the Middle East." Despite a lusty eagerness to see the equally lustful temptress who beckoned me to Israel, Doreen would have to wait. I opted for the boat to Beirut.

Chapter 12 – BEIRUT

It was Christmas Eve 1968 and somewhere in the bowels of the boat a polyglot crowd had gathered to sing Christmas carols. Their singing was being piped all over the ship. They didn't know all the words and were singing off-key. On the eve of my second Christmas away from home, the cacophonous caroling heightened my homesickness.

Things started looking up on Christmas Day, however, as we rounded the head of the peninsula on which Beirut sits. It was a beautiful, clear, crisp day. The view of the city from the sea was impressive: gleaming, glass-and-steel skyscrapers melded with venerable, arched and tiled stone buildings in the hilly cityscape. Snow-capped Mt. Lebanon, studded with picturesque villages, rose steeply behind the city almost from the water's edge. Just before we reached the port we passed a park-like area - bursting with a semi-tropical floral exuberance even in winter - which graced a seaside cliff.

The park-like area turned out to be The American University of Beirut, a major institution of higher learning for the entire Middle East since its founding by American missionaries in 1866 (Nineteen AUB grads were delegates to the signing of the United Nations Charter in 1945, probably more than those from of Oxford, Harvard, or any other university). I spent the day there, reading in the library, which to my surprise was open on Christmas. A typical American campus, it was one of the most beautiful I'd ever seen. Memories of Christmases at home faded, as it was hard to remember it was Christmas what with all the flowers in bloom. That night I slept on campus under a bush blooming in scarlet profusion.

The next evening I wandered out to the area of fancy hotels and luxury apartments which faced the sea on the other side of the peninsula. Up on a cliff at the far end of a brightly lit bay I found a rambling, abandoned hotel, not very old by the looks of it. It had a spectacular view of the city and sea. The price was right – free, since it was closed - so I checked myself into one of the cabanas by the scum-coated pool. (I later learned the hotel had been bought by a Kuwaiti who lived in the apartment building behind it so he could close it as he didn't like all the noise.)

I was sitting poolside that night, admiring the view and fantasizing the shadows into shapely, bikini-clad loungers, when I saw some bright red flashes down by the airport. Then, a few minutes later, I heard the "whoosh, whoosh" of helicopters passing overhead. Hitchhiking up into the mountains the next morning, I learned the sight and sound were courtesy of the Israelis, whose commandos had blown up a dozen or so jets of the Lebanese-owned Middle East Airlines. I'm not sure what motivated the attack; could be the Israelis just wanted to show who was boss in that part of the world.

The first people who picked me up were a young professional couple who were on their way up to their ancestral village in the mountains to visit their parents. Like so many Lebanese, both husband and wife were trilingual, able to converse freely in English, French, and Arabic. They invited me to join their family gathering - remarkable courtesy considering what our closest ally in the Middle East had just done. I got to hear a lot about what the Lebanese thought of the attack, and the steadfast ally of the attacker, over a lunch of olives, goat cheese, stuffed grape leaves, parsley salad, lamb meatballs, and other delicacies, a scrumptious meal of a couple of dozen different bite-sized items the Lebanese call a *"mezza"*. Once again I was surprised at how gracious and friendly these people could be while blaming my country for the worst sort of outrages.

"Why do you Americans let the Jews run your country?" was the lead question posed to me. I tried to explain the intricacies of American domestic politics as best I understood them, but my audience remained convinced the Jews were in control. The question would become a constant conversation opener so long as I was in the Arab world. I got so sick of it and the smug, ignorant, closed-mindedness with which my studied answer was received that eventually my stock response became "Because they do such a good job of it. Maybe you should let them run *your* country, too."

Returning to Beirut in the evening, I was let off a mile inland from my seaside lodgings. I took a bearing and headed off in the direction I guessed my objective lay. Soon I was passing through an area of muddy, narrow alleys, cinder block hovels, their tin roofs held down with stones, and the smells of too many people crammed into too little space. I noticed a man was following me. I wondered why. He didn't seem intent on mugging me. He'd already passed up many opportunities to try that. I wasn't particularly fearful as he was quite old and small. Just curious.

"What do you want? Why are you following me?" I demanded, turning and towering menacingly over him.

"*Shu btamel hoon?*" he fired back, equally forcefully, his eyes glowering at me.

He could have repeated it all night and I still wouldn't have known what he was asking. Best I could make out, he seemed to be asking me pretty much the same question I had asked him. Soon we attracted a crowd, everyone talking at once and of one voice in the hostile tone they directed at me. Many incomprehensible questions, and probably some curses, were voiced by my interlocutors, their faces near livid with rage. A sense of *déjà vu*, of another angry mob in a restaurant in Brazil, flashed through my addled mind. The crowd started coaxing me towards what they called a "police station" but which looked to me more like a communal outhouse. I was beginning to wonder how I was going to get myself out of this one.

"*Halas, muwataneen,! Halas!*"

Two young, neatly dressed Arabs had inserted themselves between me and the crowd and were addressing their compatriots. I hadn't seen such polished, self-assured persuasiveness since I watched Marie Ines tame that crowd in the student restaurant. I don't know what they said, but whatever it was it worked. The crowd calmed down and started to disperse.

"Please excuse the behavior of our neighbors," the taller of the two said, switching from Arabic to English as easily as a train switching tracks. "Everyone is very tense, very suspicious because of last night's events. You see, we are Palestinians and this is a Palestinian refugee camp."

"Oh, I see," I said, but didn't really. I didn't know what a Palestinian was or where exactly they were refugees from. It must be hard to believe I could have been so ignorant of a people whose plight is so well known today, but consider that about this same time that Golda Meier, the Israeli Prime Minister, made the provocative remark "There were no such thing as Palestinians.... They did not exist", to which the response of your average American was "Who?"

"Come. We will take you to the main road."

Khalil and Ahmed told me something about themselves as we walked along. They were university students, majoring in electrical engineering, the sort of major industrious, disadvantaged people the world over study, so much more practical than my own liberal-artsy history major. During the day they worked to support their families; at night they studied. They explained to me why they and the other Palestinians were living in Lebanon, but my background knowledge of recent Middle Eastern history was so sketchy all I could understand was that it had something to do with the creation of Israel.

"You might want to remove *that* the next time you visit a refugee camp," Khalil suggested with a wink, pointing to the American flag pinned on my backpack. I used it when hitchhiking, betting it would convey a more positive than negative image to potential lifts. It had worked well enough in Latin America, but from then on I left it *inside* my pack in this part of the world.

"Good idea!" I agreed, shaking their hands as they left me at the edge of the camp. They were the first Palestinians I'd ever met. In the years to come I would encounter many more like them, walking along some dusty road bordering a refugee camp, absorbed in some weighty technical tome. Personable, hardworking, thirsty for knowledge, they reminded me of Jews I had known growing up in more than just their looks.

I made it back to my room with a view and was just bedding down in my sleeping bag when a flashlight thrust through the paneless window of the cabana illuminated my humble abode. It was the Lebanese army. They had belatedly decided the hotel would make a good lookout post to guard against just the sort of attack which had occurred the previous night. They were more than a little surprised to find the hotel had a guest and invited me to spend the night in the army prison, an invitation I found too emphatically extended to refuse.

My "arrest" garnered me a bed for the night - hard but safe - and a breakfast of *café au lait*, bread, and jam in the morning. I was interrogated by a baffled but courteous major, while a black-suited, sunglass-bespectacled intelligence type scowled suspiciously at me from a corner. Deciding I was just some crazy Westerner doing the sort of crazy thing Westerners do, the officer let me go, with the proviso I find some other accommodations than my hotel by the sea.

Chapter 13 – GEORGE

I met George while sipping a cognac at a sidewalk cafe and watching the sexily attired Lebanese girls strut their stuff down Beirut's main shopping and gawking promenade, Hamra Street. I was celebrating having landed a job teaching at International College, a private school adjoining the AUB campus, earlier that day. George was seated at the table next to mine.

George invited me to join him and offered to treat me to dinner. After a near starvation diet the last few days because of my rapidly dwindling cash reserve, that would be my fifth meal of the day. First, breakfast courtesy of the Lebanese army. Then, on my way to search out a new place to stay, I was befriended by a Lebanese teenager who invited me back to his basement room where he fed me my second meal of the day - let's call it brunch. When, later that morning, I learned I had a job, I figured I no long had to be quite so tight in my budgeting and bought lunch. The cognac I was having when I met George was the *digestif* following a dinner I'd just completed and paid for. So I declined George's offer, explaining that I'd already eaten; but then I learned something more about Arabs. Their insistence on extending hospitality is matched by their insistent refusal to let you decline it. So I had my fifth meal of the day. I suppose it didn't do my system any harm, though I did feel a bit bloated.

74

George turned out to be a middleman in the rags trade. Despite being in his forties, he still lived with his parents, as is customary with Arab families (marriage is the only means of escape). Though Christian, he fit to a tee our caricature of a Jew: pudgy, shrewd, generous, with an affable, humorous manner he embellished with shrugs and gestures worthy of the Garment District. I enjoyed his company and he seemed to enjoy mine.

George was gay. He made this clear by an open admission, not a hand creeping up my thigh. I made it equally clear I was not. He said it didn't matter. He could accept a Platonic relationship. He only wanted to be able to gaze upon me. I became a kept man of sorts. I dined with George several times in the coming week. He lavished much needed presents on me, like a warm parka. He told me how much he loved me. I said I liked him, too.

One night George was accompanying me while I checked out prospective rooms to rent. When I first arrived in Beirut I had gone to the American University hospital to sell my blood. The going rate was $15 a pint. An orderly extracted a drop of my blood, but after testing it he informed me I didn't have enough hemoglobin in my blood for them to accept it. Dismayed not so much by the implication for my health but for my wallet, I invested one of my few remaining dollars in a bottle of iron tablets, hoping the investment would yield a fifteen-fold return. I started downing eight or ten pills a day, far more than the recommended dosage.

As the landlord opened the door to the third apartment we'd looked at that night, I felt a sharp, abdominal pain. I burst through the door and, without so much as glancing around, rushed straight to the bathroom. There, after shitting metallic little turds which clanked as they hit the side of the bowl, I felt like I was going to pass out. I came within an inhalation of calling George for help. I can only imagine what might have happened had George had me alone, weak, in the bathroom with my pants down. As it was, I recovered quickly and was able to zip up my fly unaided.

That's as close as George and I came to consummating the relationship. When, a few nights later, as we quaffed cognac at his beach-side villa, George pulled out a photo album of naked Adonises enjoying each other's bodies - a souvenir of a trip to Amsterdam - then, sidling up behind me, poked me in the rear with his hard on, I decided George's love was not as Platonic as he led me to believe. I ended the "romance" and we parted friends, I guess. I never saw him again. I missed the presents.

I found a room on my own and settled down to my job teaching English to third and fourth grade Arabs. I was proud that I was making it on my own at the second pit stop on my lap around the world and delighted at how easy it had been. Beirut seemed a good choice. It was as exciting, pleasant, and beautiful as Rio. Would the young ladies prove comparable? I could hardly wait to find out!

Chapter 14 - SAMIRA

I was walking down the corridor of International College a few months later when I saw an Arab girl entering the principal's office. "Now that's more like it!," I thought to myself, admiring her tapering calves, shapely waist, and soft, dark tresses. Imagine my surprise when the principal escorted her into my classroom a few minutes later.

"This is Samira, Ken," the principal said, introducing her. "She's studying for a teacher's certificate at AUB and will be attending your class as an observer for a few days."

By her shy, demur manner I quickly realized Samira was not one of your Beiruti girls, those Westernized offspring of Lebanese society who can hold their own in brashness and sophistication with their emulated sisters to the west. She was a real Arab. Intimidated by all I'd heard of Arab dating rituals, or the absence thereof, I didn't dare ask her out. But a week or so later, after Samira had attended my class three or four times, I saw her standing in line in the girls' cafeteria, where I sometimes ate (for some reason the food tasted better in the girls' cafeteria than the boys'). I invited her to join me at my table. Perhaps to the surprise of both of us, she did. I happened to mention I was going to the horse races that weekend and, as I would with any pretty American girl, asked if she'd like to go. She accepted, again, I think, to the surprise of both of us.

The Beirut race track was a seedy place where bony Arabians, as sad a vestige of the Arabians of yore as the Arab armies were of

Saladin's Defenders of the Faith, panted around a dusty oval while more rotund, two-legged Arabians bet, shouted, cursed, drank, and ogled my date! Samira was one of the few women at the track and the others did not look like they had been introduced to anyone's mother recently. Unsubtle, salivating men bent over to retrieve intentionally dropped items, circled below the open grandstands, and engaged in other sordid tricks in hopes of peeking up her dress. Or they uttered crude, suggestive remarks her way as we passed. It must have been very uncomfortable for her. I, of course, was totally oblivious to the whole thing, the behavioral and linguistic interactions all taking place in Arabic. The only discomfort I experienced was occasioned by the loss of a lira or two when my nag failed to finish in the money.

Miraculously, she accepted my invitation to a second date. We saw each other almost every day over the next month. She proved an adventuresome soul, weathering the icy stares of disapproving drivers as we hitchhiked up into the mountains; clinging to my neck as I swam out into the sea she was deathly afraid of at Byblos, the quaint port from which the word "bible" is derived; sneaking back into her dorm after hours when she couldn't escape, or didn't try to escape, my amorous embrace for too long.

She was, as I had guessed, a real Arab. She came from a little village in that part of Palestine called the West Bank. She had won a U. S. Agency for International Development scholarship, the first in her family to attend college. She was now a junior, majoring in biology. She was only a year younger than me, having taught for a few years prior to entering AUB.

She was a pretty little thing. In fact, she had been named Miss AID/AUB at the Christmas dance the same day I had arrived in Lebanon six month previous. Her olive skin provided the perfect setting for her satiny hair, her dark eyes flashing a look both tentative and seductive, her heart-shaped lips eternally pursed as if waiting to be kissed, her graceful, feminine way of stooping to pick things up, she reminded me of Latin American girls I had found equally beguiling.

Samira introduced me to the concept of "the village girl," as she would call herself. Often, after we had engaged in some outrageously shocking activity, like necking in the library stacks, she would exclaim "Imagine! A village girl!", as if critiquing the behavior of some other girl doing things any honorable village girl best leave to her debauched cousins in the city. When she was initially exposed to the concept of dating upon arrival at AUB, she was sure she would never engage in such a scandalous courting ritual (all of her seven brothers and sisters had arranged marriages). But the laidback, liberating ambiance of a co-ed American college worked its magic and she had been on a couple of innocent dates prior to going for it in a big way with me.

Dating Samira was different than any other dating I had ever done. There were none of the usual games: Do I let him kiss me on the first date? Do I call her back tonight or wait a week? Should I play hard to get? Samira was totally devoid of guile; her feelings for me, transparent. It was obvious she was in love with me long before she told me so. She accorded me total trust, putting her life in my hands, almost literally. I don't think she risked death for what she was doing, but she certainly faced a traumatic, life-altering confrontation with her family if they found out what she was up to. Her love was so unconditional it was frightening. It was something I was both unfamiliar with and incapable of returning in kind.

One night we were "making love" in as mutually satisfying a way as we could while preserving her virginity when I got a little too rambunctious. She ran into the bathroom to see if the ultimate misfortune had befallen her. I lay there, concerned but not really appreciating the enormity of the situation.

"I think I'm alright," she said softly as she returned to the bed, "But there was some white stuff coming out down there."

"Oh, my God," I thought to myself, "What an innocent!" Pulling her to me, I whispered "I love you."

She was the second woman I had made that profession to. The first time I had known I was not speaking true. It just seemed so natural while holding the first girl I had made love to in my arms. We were having so much fun that summer, that "Summer of Love". But when the young lady – just eighteen – returned my profession, she meant it. She wouldn't have offered up her virginity as a token of her love for me otherwise. Months later when I was in Brazil and knew I would never see her again, I agonized over whether it was better to let her go on with the delusion or to free her so she could get on with her life by confessing my lie. In the end, I confessed. I felt so guilty I swore I would never use those words again except in total sincerity.

Now I had used them again and I wondered if I really meant them this time. Samira was special for sure, but was it just an exuberant outburst inspired by a blissful, fleeting relationship or an expression of something deeper, something more lifelong? Was I opening up my heart or salving the heart of one who so desperately wanted to hear those words? I didn't know. Sometimes I found myself so self-centered I thought myself incapable of love. I suppose I wasn't the first to be troubled by such doubts.

Samira's and my romantic idyll ended with the end of the school year. She was returning to her home in Palestine for the summer and I was continuing on my way around the world. My next stop was my original destination when I left Brazil: Israel. I told Samira so and promised to visit her, the West Bank then being under Israeli control. I didn't mention Doreen, the coquette whose hot kisses had led me to the eastern end of the Mediterranean in the first place.

Chapter 15 – ISRAEL

Doreen remembered me. She invited me to stay with her and her family in their suburban Tel Aviv home. Doreen was as sassy and sexy as ever. Israeli girls enjoyed a reputation for libertinism at the time second only to the Swedes. I was looking forward to making a physical conquest of Doreen as complete as my romantic conquest of Samira.

One night after her parents had gone to bed, Doreen poked her head out her bedroom door and signaled to me to come to her room. I got up from my couch-bed in the living room and tiptoed towards her room. Not sure exactly what she had in mind, I had put on my jeans. My modesty was unnecessary for there in an easy chair on the far side of the room sat Doreen, sprawled back, attired in nothing but her bra and panties. I walked towards her with eager anticipation, but just as I got within arm's length, she raised her legs and, pressing them against my stomach, held me away from her.

We bantered back and forth, a duel of whispered taunts and innuendos meant to arouse and challenge, while she held me in that restrained position. I stroked her naked calves and tried to ease my hands up her thighs to reach the land of milk and honey, but she flicked my hands away with a deft move of her legs each time I approached the Promised Land. Then, still toying with me verbally, she slowly slid her legs down my body and began massaging my crotch with her feet. The bulge under her toes told her she had achieved the desired effect. Interpreting her pleasure-giving as an invitation, I gently spread her legs, easing them around my waist, then inched my body towards hers.

Wham! With a quick, wrenching twist of her legs she had knocked my legs out from under me and thrown me to the floor. Her full-throated laughter broke the hush of our clandestine rendezvous.

"I guess that will teach you not to mess with a poor, defenseless girl, at least not one trained by the Israeli Defense Forces!" she gloated. "Now get out of her before my parents come in to see what that thud was."

I retreated from her room like a dog, the fast shriveling thing between my legs in lieu of a tail. That humiliating episode pretty much typified my relationship with Doreen. I liked her for her brazen self-assuredness and hated her for her brazen taunting. She's the only girl I'd ever met that I felt I could rape and feel good about it. Had I, I suspect I would have found that she was, like Samira, a virgin. Her response to vestigial moral constraints demanding she preserve her unsoiled state until marriage was to make a game of it, whether to ease the pressure on herself or, as I imputed in my frustration, to humiliate the opposing gamesman just for the fun of it. Seen in this light, her behavior was to an extent forgivable; at least she observed some moral code. But it was maddening just the same.

While my stay with Doreen proved sexually unrewarding, it did provide some interesting insights into Israeli society, insights I had little expected. While in Beirut, I had met a number of resident Americans, most associated with AUB, who held views critical of Israel which were new to me. I couldn't understand where they were coming from. "Could all these nice, decent-seeming people be anti-Semitic?" I wondered. I concluded they had either lived in the Arab world too long or were mouthing sentiments they knew their Arab hosts wanted to hear to ingratiate themselves. Now I was finding maybe I should have listened more carefully to them.

The thing that struck me most about the Israelis was their haughty, racist-like attitude towards the Arabs. The response of the military governor of the West Bank town of Jeneen, with whom I was hitching a ride, when I inquired as we entered the town "Is this Jeneen?" was typical. "Smells like Jeneen, doesn't it?" he sneered. He and most of the other Israelis I encountered were quick to ascribe the crowds of idle men standing on street corners to the Arabs' innate laziness. All that was lacking were separate water fountains for me to believe I'd stumbled on some Jewish version of Mississippi. Thinking of the urbane, hard-working, intelligent Arabs I'd known in Beirut, both Lebanese and Palestinian, I would have found their superior attitude laughable were it not so tragic for the Palestinians. I came to believe that, in the long run, it was likely to prove equally tragic for the Israelis.

Not used to hearing Jews sound like Nazi storm-troopers and believing the Israelis, like all of us, adopted prejudices which serve the psychological needs imposed by the situation in which we find ourselves, I took a new interest in "The Arab-Israeli Conflict". I searched out the local USIA library and began reading up on the history of the conflict. I was amazed not so much by what I learned but by what a different light I saw the narrative in than I had prior to coming to Israel.

There, in the sort of textbooks I might have studied in high school, was described how in 1890 a non-practicing Austrian Jew named Theodore Herzl had written a book, *The Jewish State*, in which he argued that the Jews needed their own country to escape inevitable persecution; how a small group of ardent believers, labeled "Zionists", had begun colonizing Palestine, while well-connected Jews convinced the British government to throw its support behind "the establishment in Palestine of a national home for the Jewish people"; how between the world wars the Arabs, Zionists, and British played a three-cornered game of tug-of-war as both the Arabs and Zionists sought to oust the British, while each eyed the other with suspicion as to what their long-term goal was; how a massive influx of Jews from Nazi-threatened Europe arrived in the country before and after the Second World War; how the newly-organized United Nations proposed a partition plan for Palestine in 1947 which awarded half of Palestine – and the better half at that! – to the Jews though they only constituted a third of Palestine's population; how the British withdrew and fighting immediately broke out between the Palestinians and the Zionists; how the Zionists succeeded in defeating not only the Palestinians but the armies of the neighboring Arab states and created the state of Israel; how hundreds of thousands of Palestinians had fled their homes during the fighting and were now languishing in refugee camps in the West Bank, Lebanon, Jordan, the Gaza Strip, and elsewhere.

Reading the chronology of events, what I saw now that I hadn't seen before was the native population of Palestine. I felt like the idealistic, ardent, early Zionist who, when he learned there were people in Palestine, exclaimed "But I thought it was a desert. Then what we are doing is wrong!" I thought back to the images of brave Israelis defending their homes against savage, marauding Arabs I had been brought up on and how it never dawned on me that the Israelis lived in fort-like kibbutzim for the same reason our West was peppered with forts: because we and they had stolen somebody else's land. The Israelis had good reason to adopt a racist attitude towards the Arabs to soothe their psyches.

In the euphoria following the 1967 war, the Israelis had become an even more stiff-necked people. But I suspected they would find the Arabs were no Indians. The Zionist movement seemed to me to be the last hurrah of a Western expansionism which had carried Europeans to the farthest corners of the globe in triumph but which had been in full retreat in the 20th century. The Zionists had succeeded through the fortuitous meshing of Great Power geostrategic interests, a tragedy of biblical proportions befalling the Jews of Europe, and the magnified importance of the Middle East with the discovery of oil there; but, in the long run, I saw the Israelis sharing the fate of other Western colonialists. One way or another, through peaceful means or war, the Israelis would eventually succumb to the ineluctable resurgence of the Arabs.

These thoughts did not come to me all at once from reading a book. All I understood initially was that I had been duped. The insularity of my native land, separated as it was from the rest of mankind by two oceans, and its possession of a machinery of public opinion-molding in its media which would be the envy of any totalitarian state, had led me to view the situation upside down. Victim became victimizer; oppressor, the oppressed. But if you hold that my transformed perception of the Arab-Israeli conflict was not due to any great intellectual awakening but to my feelings for one sweet, Palestinian village girl, I won't dispute you (Better that than being labelled "anti-Semitic"!). I don't believe it, because I credit myself with an objectivity that cannot be swayed by even such a powerful, personal factor, but I can see why you may.

Critical as I am of the Israelis' aggressive, racist, sanctimonious ways, I try not to consider them evil (well, except maybe for that prick-tease Doreen!). I subscribe to the Nietzschean dictum that there is no evil in the world, only ignorance. How else to explain the anomaly of our most revered founding fathers practicing slavery while solemnly proclaiming the equality of men? Were they being hypocritical, evil? No more than the rest of us, in my opinion. Like all of us, their beliefs were shaped by the times in which they lived. I can believe they sincerely thought slavery was a blessing for the African, lifting him out of a pagan savagery. Who are we, two centuries removed and subject to our own ignorance, to judge them? We are all more ignorant than knowing, and in that ignorance capable of actions which may well be seen by future generations as evil.

Chapter 16 – BEIT JALA

My guides, a gang of jabbering boys, led me up the cobbled street to Samira's house. There were no addresses in Beit Jala and no need for them. Everyone knew everyone else; indeed, most everyone was related to most everyone else! Before I even reached her door I think the whole town knew an *ajnabiya* (foreigner) had come to visit Samira. The old ladies of the village must have been atingle at the prospect of the juicy gossip that would ensue, enough to fill weeks of idle chatter round the well.

Beit Jala is a classic Palestinian village. Its stolid, earth-toned houses, sprinkled hodgepodge across the olive-green slopes of the Judean hills, speak of antiquity, of permanence, of timelessness. Just a stone's throw from Bethlehem, Beit Jala is, like its more famous neighbor, a Christian town. This is not to say no Muslims live there; simply that most of the residents worship the little fellow born across the way. When Samira was born, the village was part of mandate Palestine, administered by the British, After the Arab defeat in Israel's War of Independence it had been annexed, along with the rest of the West Bank, by King Hussein's Jordan. Now, two years after the Six Day War, it was still part of Jordan officially but under Israeli occupation.

Tears welled up in Samira's eyes at the sight of me. I don't know whether she had mentioned me to her family, but, even if she had, it was clear she was going to have a lot of explaining to do. Her mother and the two siblings still at home were all very gracious but as ill-at-ease as I was, this not being an everyday event for any of us. The first thing Samira did was whisk me off to her aunt's house, as hers was the only house in the family with a bathtub.

The contrast between Doreen and Samira and Doreen's family and Samira's could not have been starker. I'd left the familiar ambiance of a suburban home with all the modern conveniences for a two-room hand-hewn stone house - far older than anything on the National Register of Historic Places - where the mother squatted by a kerosene stove to cook. I'd left a family where two working parents and a self-reliant daughter led independent lives which only crossed now and then for the smothering embrace of a family where almost every moment of their waking lives were spent together, every joy and every sorrow shared. Most significantly, I'd left one brash, conniving hussy for a woman who was all guilelessness and surrender.

Samira's family was typical of the village. The mother, widowed at twenty-eight with eight kids, had somehow raised her brood to adulthood through hard work and the mutual support provided by an extended family. Poverty had forced her to put Samira and two of her siblings in a local orphanage, run by a religious group from our Midwest, for four years when they were young. It's hard to imagine what a traumatic experience this must have been for such a close-knit family, the mother as well as the kids. Now Samira's mom was reaping the fruits of her labor. All but the three youngest were successfully married off, the married ones being scattered around the globe in Canada, the United States, Jordan, and Kuwait.

Samira's émigré brothers and sisters had not been driven from their homeland by Zionist usurpation, as I might have wanted to believe with my newfound sympathy for the Palestinian cause. They had simply done what young people in impoverished countries all over the world did: moved to where the jobs were. In fact, I couldn't see where the Israeli occupation had made much of a change in Beit Jala one way or the other. There may have been more soldiers in evidence under King Hussein's rule! That potentate – his family, the Hashemites, having been awarded the throne of Transjordan by the British as a consolation prize when the Hashemites were thrown out of Arabia by a rival clan, the Saudis - had not done much to inspire the loyalty of his Palestinian subjects during the twenty year he ruled the West Bank. Many Beit Jalans shrugged at the outcome of the recent war, feeling they had just traded an incompetent, aloof ruler for rule by equally aloof foreigners who at least got the mail delivered in a timely manner.

Samira's mother loved to tell the story of how she was caught on the wrong side of the Jordan River when the war broke out. She had to sneak across the river in the dead of night to get back to Beit Jala, just as Palestinian guerrillas with less peaceful intents were doing every night. In telling the story she showed no animosity towards the Israelis. She treated the war as if it was a natural catastrophe, like an earthquake or a hurricane, the sort of calamity common folk like her were always having to suffer through, while praying they would survive it all.

Samira's family had so far not been greatly affected by the trauma their fellow countrymen had experienced. They had been spared the refugee experience. Their lives had not been radically altered by either the war of 1948 or that of 1967, not in the way the lives of Palestinians driven from their homes and now living in refugee camps had been.

"This must explain Samira's surprisingly apolitical attitude," I surmised. She seemed to feel no loyalty to anything beyond her family. Coming from a country where patriotism assumes the fervid aspect of a religion, I found this shocking. In light of the national catastrophe her country had gone through - now twice - it was beyond shocking. It was contemptible.

Placed in historical perspective, however, it made sense. The people of Palestine have been conquered by invading armies so many times they've stopped counting. Egyptians, Babylonians, Hebrews, Romans, Greeks, Muslims, Crusaders, Turks, Brits - all swept through, planted their flag, levied their taxes, demanded obedience, then been swept aside by the next band of conquering heroes. Not a history to inspire loyalty to whomever happened to be the occupying power in Palestine at any one time. The people of Palestine, Samira and her family amongst them, had responded in a logical, sensible manner: welcome the new arrivals and see what you can sell them.

In fact, this has been the attitude of most people in most places throughout history. The modern phenomenon of citizen participation in their government and hence mass loyalty to that government is an aberration. The normal relation between governors and governed has been an antagonistic one. The only contact the ruled had with their ruler was through the royal tax collector sent around to collect a proportion of the people's harvest and the recruiter sent to dragoon young men into the royal army. The common folk might wave enthusiastically as their king, emperor, or sultan paraded by in full regalia or tell tales of the heroism of past rulers to their kids, but as far as actually sacrificing for their ruler, that was the duty of his soldiers and courtesans, i.e., those who benefited from his largesse. If, through circumstances beyond the ruler's control, like a drought, or the result of his own incompetence, like losing a war, the ruler became too exacting – stealing too much of their harvest or drafting too many sons and husbands, then it was time for a peasant revolt.

All this changed with the Industrial Revolution. Relations between the ruler and the ruled became complex, pervasive, and close. Advances in transportation brought not only the capital city closer to the citizenry, but citizens closer to one another, facilitating a sense of commonality, of nationhood. The revolution in agricultural production freed the rural population to move to the cities and man the factories. The need for an educated work force to man the new machines led to an expansion of literacy, which led to an ubiquitous news media which could shape, as much as inform, public opinion. The complexity of industrialized society demanded more intervention by the government in the lives of the common man which led inexorably to the common man demanding more of a say in his government. With rights came duties, including rallying to the country's call in time of war. The surpluses generated by bountiful harvests and humming factories enabled the maintenance of militaries on a scale the world had never known. In a word, mass production led to mass everything: mass transport, mass education mass media, mass consumption, mass bureaucracies, mass militaries.

And, thus, an insignificant island with bad weather off the northwest coast of the European mainland – an outland throughout all previous history, came to rule an empire on which the sun never set. A numerically insignificant band of industrious merchants, well-motivated bureaucrats, and well-trained and armed soldiers conquered, by both peaceful and violent means, whole subcontinents. They were able to do this by inducing subordination in native rulers by offering them a share of the spoils of global commerce – tempting emoluments, business partnerships – and by offering to the native populace the tangible benefits of progress: modern medicine, railroads, cheap consumer goods. Facilitating acquiescence in their subordination was the ruler's realization that their subjects were by and large indifferent to the ruler's fate. The native rulers were almost as foreign to their erstwhile people as were the new rulers from across the sea. For the rulers to count on the ruled's support in fending off the foreign interlopers would have been a breach of the age-old, informal code which governed rights and duties of ruler and ruled. A ruler who demanded first night rights over the brides in his domain (*Droit du seigneur*) couldn't expect his subjects to rally to his cause repulsing the foreigners.

Similar countries going through similar revolutions acquired similar empires, and so the West came to dominate the East. In Palestine, the West achieved dominance as well, but with a twist. Supplementing – in some ways complementing – British rule was the influx of well-funded, well-organized, well-motivated Zionists pouring into Palestine one shipload after another, The response of the Palestinian ruling class as often as not was to sell the land for the Zionists to build their kibbutzim on, then move to Beirut to live comfortably on the proceeds as things heated up back home in consequence of their land sales. The Palestinian peasant, indifferent to being rule by robed sheikh or pith-helmeted Brit, remained focused on his family and village. He could not see the danger over the horizon, knowing little about the ideology-driven ambitions of the Zionists or the plight of Jews in Europe. He simply looked on the newest arrivals as customers for his produce or employers offering good-paying jobs.

And so it came to pass that the Israelis, the late-blooming offspring of the triumphant West, were successful in driving the

Palestinians from their land. If the Palestinians are ever to regain their land they will have to adopt the mindset of the Israelis, the mindset of modern countries. They must discover what bonds them to other Palestinians, refugees or not, find patriotic leaders capable of mobilizing the nation on the basis of that bond, and be willing to sacrifice for their country, as my fellow countrymen were doing – or believed they were doing – in Vietnam. The day Samira - goaded by insults from Israeli border guards on her way to or from AUB or by her village lands being expropriated by fanatical Zionist settlers - became aware of and rallied round those who shared her tongue, her land, her history, and her culture would be the day the Palestinians came of age as a nation.

But that was not my immediate concern. I was more interested in the bond Samira might feel towards one with whom the only bond she shared was an occasional embrace. I discovered that, despite boasting a dozen words for each part of the camel, Arabic doesn't seem to have a single word for "privacy." If I withdrew into myself, as I sometimes do, Samira and her family would badger me until I rejoined the party, concerned that I was sick or that they had done something wrong, when all I wanted was to be alone for a while. Needless to say, Samira and I were never alone. The only time I was alone with Samira in the three days I spent with her family was when we were touring Jerusalem with her younger brother as chaperone and Samira convinced him to let us go inside the Dome of the Rock – the beautiful, gold-topped shrine marking where Mohammed ascended into heaven - unescorted. Finding a secluded nock behind some pillars in this the third holiest site in Islam, my libido took over and I gave Samira a passionate kiss, hidden just enough from the rows of worshippers repeating their afternoon prayers.

"I have to leave you, my darling," I whispered to her, more caught up in the moment than I would have believed possible of me.

"I know," she said softly, with the demur manner and downcast eyes which brought out whatever compassion was in me.

"I'll be back though, in a year or two." I meant it, at least at that moment.

"I'll wait for you, Ken," she promised, raising her tear-filled eyes to mine.

Chapter 17 – GOLAN HEIGHTS

A few days later I was hitchhiking towards the Golan Heights, the lofty plateau overlooking the Sea of Galilee which had been part of Syria prior to the 1967 war but was now occupied by Israel. I was headed to a kibbutz I'd heard about on the Golan. It wasn't a normal kibbutz, the kind American Jews send their kids to for a summer. It was a semi-communal attempt to build a ski resort on the slopes of Mount Hermon, formerly out of reach for Israelis.

I was at my post, standing by the roadside down in the valley below the heights, thumb out, when an old man lugging two heavy buckets appeared up the road. Heading in my direction, he stopped fifty yards away to rest. I knew I should offer to help him but it was getting late in the day, there hadn't been many cars along, and I wanted to make the kibbutz before nightfall. Then he stopped right beside me. With his white moustache, stooped manner, and twinkling eyes, he looked like Pinocchio's Guiseppe.

"Good afternoon, young man," he said cheerily, in English that was only slightly accented. "Would you mind helping me carry this water to my home. It's just off the road a bit, up that little path."

Cornered that way, I couldn't very well refuse. I lifted one bucket while he led the way carrying the other.

"Where are you headed?" he asked between breaths. I tried to place his accent. It was different from the guttural accent of the typical Israeli, but I couldn't place it.

"To the Golan," I replied.

"Oh, you won't find much up there. Just some deserted villages," he said matter of factly.

"Is that so? The Arabs all fled during the war, did they?"

"Not exactly fled," he went on equally matter of factly. "They were driven out. Once the Israelis won control of the Heights, they cleared out the villages. Rounded up the people and took them to the front lines where they forced them to cross over into Syria. Those who refused, they shot. That convinced the others."

Down as I was by that time on the Israelis, I still found this hard to believe. "I never heard anything about that!" I interjected.

"I know," he said. "They call it 'The Six Day War', but up here it's known as 'The Twelve Day War'. That's how long it took the Israelis to rid the Golan of Arabs. Believe me, I know. I watched the tanks go up this very road, heard the fighting day after day, talked to the soldiers as they returned wounded from the front. The Arabs put up much stiffer resistance than most people think!"

The way he told the story gave it the ring of truth. When I thought about it, it made sense. The Israelis certainly didn't want to have to rein herd over a bunch of hostile Arabs and it's not easy to get an Arab to leave his native village. Maybe this explained what caused the Palestinians to "flee" their homes during the 1948 war.

"Are you an Israeli?" I asked as we put the buckets down outside his home: two dilapidated shacks, one housing a few half-starved animals, the other crammed with odds and ends.

"No," he replied with a slight chuckle. "Hungarian. My name is Paul Horvath." He extended his hand and I felt the strength of a laborer in it as I shook it.

"Does that name mean anything to you?" he asked.

"No, it doesn't," I confessed. "Should it?"

"It once meant a great deal to the people of Hungary," he said with feeling. "It's the name of the former royal family of Hungary, of which I am a proud though destitute member."

I didn't know whether to believe him or not. It didn't really matter. Even if he weren't royalty, he clearly was raised in better surroundings than his current abode. He was well-read, articulate, and had the calm self-assuredness of one who had once commanded respect. That night, after I had accepted his invitation to spend the night, he read to me from six of the hundred or so Bibles cluttering up his small domain, each Bible seemingly in a different language.

We pooled our resources to fashion a humble meal. To his farm-fresh eggs and homemade bread I added a tin of sardines and some cheap processed cheese featuring a laughing French cow. After dinner, I learned more about His Royal Highness over a glass of tea.

"I came here before the war" he began, then, noticing my puzzled look, clarified, "No, not the Six Day War; the Second World War. I wanted to live in the land of our Lord and Saviour, Jesus Christ."

"Oh brother, a Jesus freak!" I thought to myself. I imagined so much more interesting things that might have caused him to leave his homeland – a tragic love affair, a palace coup, revolutionaries in the streets.

"I bought a nice farm. I had money back then. What you see is all that's left of it," he said with a sigh. "The Israelis took it all. They wanted my land for a kibbutz. I wouldn't sell, so they just took it. They keep offering me money, but I won't take it. I've been fighting them in the courts for years. And I will continue to fight them! I don't want money. I want my farm back."

Looking at his muscular frame and set jaw I bet he was a tough adversary. He'd have to be to take on the Israelis. They weren't in the habit of returning stolen land. Quite the contrary!

"All I was able to save are these two buildings and a right of way to the road, the path we came down. The kibbutz lets me get water from them. Very generous, considering they've cut off my access to my own wells! They tried to be friendly at first, but it didn't work. How could I forgive them? I hate the Israelis!" he concluded with vehemence, then corrected himself, "No, I hate the Zionists."

The next night found me crouched in a trench in the center of Camp Aspenowitz, as we foreign volunteers jokingly dubbed the kibbutz, an Uzi slung across my chest. There wasn't much happening in the way of work because of the threat of guerrilla attack from across the nearby border with Lebanon, so all I had to do to earn my cot and three just passable meals a day was a couple of hours of guard duty each night. The Israeli soldiers officially guarding the kibbutz gave us some rudimentary training in handling Uzi submachine guns, then had us take our stations in the trenches which, along with three rings of barbed wire, constituted the camp's defenses.

Sitting up there watching the flash of firefights taking place all up and down the Jordan Valley, I thought of Paul Horvath. And of Samira. I thought of quiet Arab villages and bustling Jewish cities; of marauding armies, some with swastikas, some with the Star of David; of half-starved refugees, some behind the barbed wire of concentration camps, some, the shield of the United Nations Relief and Works Agency for Palestine Refugees. I thought of man's inhumanity to man. I wanted to cry, but I was too scared.

I was scared the Palestinians would attack the kibbutz I was armed to defend. What would I do if they did? I suspected there wouldn't be occasion to explain to the protagonists on either side that I was just an innocent bystander, meaning no one any harm. I certainly didn't want to shoot Palestinians. I would much prefer to turn my gun on the Israelis who provided my weapon. But I didn't really want to shoot them, either. But what if it became to a matter of self-defense – kill or be killed?

Fortunately, I never found out the answer to that question. There was no attack that night. A month later I read in the *International Herald Tribune* that the kibbutz had been attacked. Someone had carelessly left a bulldozer outside the barbed wire perimeter and the guerrillas had blown it up. But by then I was far away to the east, continuing my circumambulation. I didn't think much more of Camp Aspenowitz, but my mind did often return to a certain village in Palestine and the dusky maiden who lived there.

Chapter 18 – KISMET

My plan - and I use the term loosely - was to travel across South Asia to the Far East, get a job teaching English, maybe in Japan; then, with funds replenished, cross the Soviet Union on the trans-Siberian railroad and work my way down through the Balkans back to Beirut. The plan satisfied two of my wishes: one, to continue my travels, and, two, to see Samira again. But my plans were nearly shot through twice, and then dealt the *coup de grace* in Iran.

The first near fatal blow occurred in Turkey. I was on the Hippy Oriental Express – the road from Istanbul to New Delhi – down which thousands of young Western pilgrims trekked, dropping out, as they put it, of the suffocating, antiseptic world of conformity and convenience they'd grown up in hopes of finding spiritual enlightenment – and cheap grass – in the exotic, immutable East. That wasn't exactly my quest, but it was nice to have the company of English-speakers after many miles on roads less traveled.

I had given up on hitchhiking in eastern Turkey. Not because the traffic along the dusty roads in that part of the world was sparse, but because it was non-existent! I switched to that most glorious form of conveyance ever invented by the mind of man: the train. Not some chrome and glass, lickety-split, smooth as glass bullet train, but those smoke-belching, coal-guzzling, rusting steeds of the Age of Steam typical of the Third World.

I was in the dining car as we clickety-clacked across eastern Anatolia. The cars former elegance was faded now, but, unlike the denigrated, underfunded trains of my native land, there was cloth on the tables and weighty, sparkling tableware on the cloth. Having had my breakfast, I was idling away the miles in the pleasant company of a scruffy young British couple and a major in the Turkish army. We were approaching the next stop, so I decided it would be prudent to head back to the car in which my things were still spread out on the seat willy-nilly to see that nothing mysteriously disappeared. My car was the last car on the train. Or had once been. The train now ended one car short of mine.

A frantic interrogation of the conductor, through the medium of the Turkish major, revealed that my car had been disconnected at the last station, Erzincan, some fifty miles behind us now. The unapologetic conductor pointed out that he had announced that's what was going to happen several times. How could I have missed it? Yes, indeed, how, what with my fluent Turkish! The conductor could only suggest I get off at the next station and catch a train back to Erzincan.

The next stop turned out to be no more than a whistle stop, but there was a train headed back in the direction I hastened to go waiting on a siding for us to pass. The only snag was it was a freight train. Suspecting that in the laid-back Third World a little formality like the fact that type of train was not authorized to carry passengers would not prevent a person in need from being able to hitch a ride, I had the major scribble a quick note in Turkish explaining my plight and prepared to leap from our train as soon as it stopped.

The freight was already starting its lumbering, screeching departure before my train had even stopped. I saw what looked like a conductor standing in the open door of a boxcar towards the front of the train and ran in his direction. I waved the major's note at him while I ran alongside the still slow-moving train and tried to climb aboard. The conductor shoved me out with a torrent of indignant Turkish and shooed me away.

I stood there watching the train slowly pull away, fuming. I had waited half a day to catch the train that brought me this far. If I missed this train, I doubted I would get back to Erzincan before my things had traded hands several times in the local bazaar. Without really making a conscious decision, I began running alongside the train and leaped onto the ladder on the end of a car a few short of the caboose. The conductor, who had laughed mockingly at me as I stood helpless beside the departing train, was now waving his fist at me and letting out another stream of prime Anatolian invective.

I hung on for dear life as the train picked up speed and began rattling from side to side. I perched like that for twenty or thirty miles, until the train stopped again to let another train pass. I ran up to the boxcar with the angry conductor once again. He read my note this time and, moved by pity or just not caring much one way or the other, he grudgingly let me climb up beside him. By the time we got back to Erzincan we were as good friends as no two words of a language in common and a cultural divide spanning continents could make us.

As we reached the station at Erzincan I could see my car sitting unattached on a siding. I ran to it, not really expecting to find my things, and I didn't. A feeling of disappointment and despair was followed by a curious sense of relief. I felt like now my fate had been sealed. I would no longer have to agonize over the decision whether to continue with my travels or return home and face the music. I had no choice, what with my passport included in the things I'd lost. The mental weight being lifted from my shoulders felt good.

You see when I visited Doreen in Israel I received two bundles of mail. One was letters from family and friends written shortly after I'd left Brazil, when I thought Israel was my destination and so had given Doreen's home as my next mailing address. The second bundle was letters sent eight months later, around the time I left Beirut, when, again, my next address was Doreen's. In each bundle was a letter from my sister Martha telling me the FBI had just contacted the family and said I was in big trouble but if I came back immediately and joined the army all would be forgiven. The fact that these two letters, written eight months apart, were almost identical in content provided me bemused confirmation that my original supposition I could put off the draft thing for a while without penalty was correct. (Less satisfying was the news that my next younger brother had dropped out of Dartmouth and, having lost his student deferment, was now in Vietnam.)

But the reassurance was belated, as I had come to view my decision to delay conscription in a changed light. I was no longer intent on postponing my military service. I now knew I would never accept to be drafted, not for Vietnam anyway. This new conviction caused me to view myself as the FBI did, as a fugitive from the law, not just some crafty shirker off on a lark. Years later I would learn how timely my change of perspective was, for the U.S. Government had undergone a corresponding change in its attitude towards me. When I failed to show up for induction after the third warning, the FBI had turned my case over to the U.S. Attorney who indicted me on two counts of draft evasion on July 31, 1969 - just about the time I was reading those near identical letters from my sister in Doreen's living room.

So, when I realized my backpack - and passport - was gone, I resigned myself to the fact that my globetrotting days were over. Despite not knowing about the indictment at that time, because I had adopted the mentality of a fugitive, I suspected that if I entered an American embassy to apply for a new passport I would be immediately clapped in irons and shipped back to the States. And I couldn't travel far without a passport.

As I dejectedly got down from the railcar, unburdened by my pack or further responsibility for my future, two Turkish teenagers grabbed me and with much excited jabbering dragged me towards the station baggage room. There, before my unbelieving eyes, was my backpack, as safe as if it had been misplaced at a family reunion. I was elated, then I felt truly ashamed. I had recently broken my long-standing policy of not making generalizations about whole nations of people and decided I really didn't like the Turks. Now, the fallacy of stereotyping a nationality - a mistake we world travelers are wont to make - was brought embarrassingly home to me.

I thanked the station manager and the kids profusely as they beamed with pride over their competence and honesty, then settled down on a bench to await the evening train east. It pulled in around midnight, six hours late. There was the usual hustle and bustle as the awaiting throng jostled and pushed to get on as if it were the last train out of Krakow before the blitz. Amazingly, I found an unoccupied compartment. Spreading my sleeping bag out on the bench seat on one side of the compartment, I quickly crawled in, vowing not to give up an inch of space no matter how many Turks, with their oversized bundles, whining babies, and cackling farm animals, crammed into the compartment. So much for my gratitude for the kindness shown me by other Turks earlier that day!

Pretending to be asleep, I happened to open one eye and noticed that the wallet in which I carried my passport, traveler's checks, and a few other documents was missing from the pocket on my backpack in which I carried them. The emotional rollercoaster of the morning when I had found my backpack missing - despair, followed by relief - swept over me again. But then a third emotion - defiance - hit me. Leaving my things in the compartment, I pushed my way off the train through the boarding masses and ran to the baggage room which had yielded such good news in the morning. No such luck this time. No one had turned in a lost wallet.

I paced desperately up and down the station platform, trying to think of what to do next, knowing the train could pull out any minute. I laughed at the irony that having run so far and so well, my fate had now been determined by a bedraggled, probably barefoot, petty thief in a dusty, forlorn town in the middle of nowhere. Bemusement was followed by anger and anger by inspiration.

I whipped a hundred lira note, worth about ten dollars, out of my pocket and, waving it aloft, began walking up and down the platform shouting "Passport!" It had occurred to me that, unless the person who stole my wallet was a six foot one, hazel-eyed, sandy-haired, smiling doofus planning a trip abroad, he probably didn't have much use for my passport. I knew that "passport", thanks to the peripatetic French, was a near universally understood word. I hoped the thief would get the idea and gladly exchange my passport for the banknote. Hell, in return for the passport, I'd gladly countersign the traveler's checks for him as well!

Discouraged but not dissuaded when several people came up to offer me change for my hundred lira, I continued my chant, and, sure enough, after another minute or two a grubby little Turk, his tough, rounded features reminiscent of a Mongol marauder, appeared out of nowhere with my wallet in his hand. I took the wallet, withholding the reward until I had a chance to confirm that the passport was still inside. It was, though the traveler's checks weren't. Sure the grinning Tartar before me was an accomplice in the crime, I stuffed the banknote back in my pocket and hopped quickly on the train. I'd just gotten back to my compartment when it started to pull out. Out the window I could see the disappointed ragamuffin running alongside the train, maligning my ancestry while futilely throwing rocks at the window.

The second time my fate was almost sealed also involved a late night boarding of a crowded train at a remote station, this time in Iraq. Older and at least somewhat wiser, I now carried the wallet with my passport in my front pants pocket, figuring no one could dislodge it from there without me being aware of it. I was wrong. As I took my seat after fighting my way through the throng of Arabs, the missing press of the thick billfold against my thigh told me I had lost my wallet – and passport - once again.

I knew the routine now. Grabbing a large denomination note from my pocket, I walked up and down the aisle from car to car, calling out "Passport! Passport!" But it didn't work this time. All I got were curious stares. As the train pulled out, I slumped into a seat, and contemplated my fate once again.

"What problem have you?" the Arab seated next to me asked in intelligible, if ungrammatical, English. He seemed like a nice, respectable type, dressed as he was in European-style clothes and smiling sympathetically.

I explained that my wallet had been stolen. He conveyed this information in Arabic to the whole car, which was eagerly waiting to learn what my strange behavior was all about. It was an open type car, with rows of seats, not compartments. Perhaps needing to commiserate with someone, anyone, I went on to tell him the whole story, how my passport was in the wallet, how I had fled my country, refusing to be sent to Vietnam, and if I had to get a new passport, I would be sent back home to be imprisoned. All this he translated for the car, who listened in rapt attention. Two years abroad had taught me that most people who live on the other side of that rose-colored glass dome from under which we Americans gaze out upon the world were repulsed by what we were doing in Vietnam. I hoped my heartrending tale might move the thief to compassion.

Shortly after the translation ended, the rapt silence was pierced by the sound of an Arab, a young man squatting in the doorway at the end of the car, breaking into song. I'd always said that, if I ever acquired a taste for Arab music, I'd know I'd been in the Arab world too long. Well, I hadn't been there too long. It still sounded like unmelodic caterwauling to me. But the audience seemed to like it.

When he finished serenading us, the crooner stood up and exited the car. After a short pause, several people started pointing excitedly at the floor near where he had been squatting. There, in plain sight was my wallet. I ran back and, picking it up, checked that my passport was still inside. As I waved it over my head, the car broke out in applause. I returned to my seat with a sheepish grin and many heartfelt *shukran*'s (Thank you).

In Teheran, a week or two later, my luck finally ran out. I was traveling in the company of two Filipinos, about the only Third Worlders I'd encountered traveling in the manner of us Western vagabonds. I looked so disreputable after a week on the road and my companions perhaps being considered disreputable no matter how natty their appearance, we were turned away by the more fastidious dumps budget travelers stayed in and were forced to take a room in a really down-and-out place. Its courtyard was filled with a gaggle of lounging, stoned, space cadets whom I would have taken for dead had not the need to get up and urinate occasionally moved them.

Back in Beirut I had purchased two ten-tola solid gold bars, each about the size of a Snickers. It was a free market there, but not in India, where I was headed, and I'd heard I could get twice as much for them there. As I traveled across Asia, the bars were hidden deep within my backpack if the pack was on my back; otherwise they nestled securely in my pants pocket. But those bars were heavy! So in

Teheran I decided to risk leaving them in the backpack while I toured the city. When I got back to the hotel, of course, they were gone.

I was devastated. Those two bars represented most of my remaining travel money. I'd never get to the Far East now. And no street urchin or yodeling passenger appeared on the scene to save me this time. I wandered the streets of Teheran in a daze, almost in tears. Fate had dealt me yet another staggering blow. But was it Fate? Or had I written my destiny with my own hand? Was it simply carelessness that led me to leave those gold bars in an unlocked room, shared with near strangers, in a dingy hotel full of penniless potheads; or had an unconscious desire to be done with it, to know the sort of relief I had experienced in Turkey when I found my passport was missing and thought it was all over, impelled me to be so careless? Who can say? I was reminded of a quatrain I'd read recently, composed by a Persian poet, mathematician, and wine connoisseur named Omar Khayyam:

> The Moving Finger writes; and having writ,
> Moves on; nor all your Piety nor Wit
>   Shall lure it back to cancel half a Line;
>   Nor all your Tears wash out a Word of it.

Chapter 19 – BENARES

The pariah kite perched majestically atop the temple, looking down in apparent contempt at the lesser beings teeming below. Then, something caught its gaze. With a swift, kamikaze-like descent it dove to the street below, snatched up a scurrying mouse in its talons, and carried its prey back to its crenelated lair. The gaunt-faced zombies shuffling through the streets paid it not the slightest attention. Nor did they look up to see blood discolor the pastel plaster of the parapet as the kite tore the life out of the hapless rodent. Death was a commonplace here.

I was in Benares, the Hindus holy city on the Ganges. It is here pious Hindus come to die, to be cremated on the banks of the holy river and have their ashes scattered in its sacred waters. Death and dying is never far from one's thoughts anywhere in India. The whole subcontinent is one despair-inducing panorama of human suffering, forever but one failed monsoon away from mass starvation. But in Benares death is tangible, pungent, overwhelming. Living, breathing skeletons, some in tattered rags, some in sacredly tinted robes, mill about the streets, from appearances starving themselves either because a lifetime's savings ran out paying the cost of the train ticket and the prepaid funeral pyre or simply to hasten their release from this Vale of Tears.

The beggars, in no great hurry themselves to cross that last frontier, add their horror to the already depressing scene. The *crème de la crème* of India's beggary, *in toto* the finest in the world, flock to Benares in hopes of partaking of the philanthropy of some rich Brahmin demonstrating his piety in one final ostentatious act before passing over into that other world that knows no castes. Malformed limbs - some natural, some contrived - puss-filled sores, glazed stares, every grotesque feature accentuated for marketing purposes like the grocer-polished sheen on an apple, cry out for pity, and spare change.

"Suits my mood perfectly," I thought as I wended my way through the crowd towards the river. I was reveling in self-pity. I felt it unfair that I should have this draft thing constricting my options for the future. I resented my friends back home who had put it behind them so easily – an old football injury exaggerated by a sympathetic doctor, being the only surviving son of a World War II vet, never-ending graduate school on Dad's account. I resented the Canadians I met in my travels who had no such "obligation" hanging over their heads. Hell, in Tunisia I'd even met some South Vietnamese students who were happily going about their lives with no fear of conscription.

Then I thought of my brother and others like him, putting their lives on the line in Vietnam. I thought how happy they would be to be sitting on the banks of the Ganges surrounded only by peaceful death. I did not feel guilty about not being there, slugging it out by their side. I'd resolved that moral issue long before, as had an increasing number of Americans who saw the war as a tragic mistake at best, a despicable crime less generously. Just a month earlier a quarter million people - and not just the young, the marginalized, the draftable, but ministers, college presidents, housewives, businessmen - had marched in Washington in opposition to the war. No, I just commiserated with my brother and his comrades in arms as fellow young men who were in a worse situation than my own.

I thought about other young men making a sacrifice of a different sort by challenging the draft and going to prison as a consequence. My own resistance, if you could call it that, seemed so wishy-washy by comparison – flitting about the globe, fixated on getting laid, whining because I occasionally had to sleep out in the rain or couldn't get a hot shower. If I was capable of any honor, I reprimanded myself, I would return to the United States, take my stand, and face the consequences.

My thoughts were a jumbled kaleidoscope of irresolution, complicated now by a new option. In Istanbul, two months earlier, I had received another letter ominously marked FOR OFFICIAL BUSINESS ONLY, but this time the return address was not my draft board but the Congress of the United States of America! As I nervously opened the envelope, I envisioned a personal letter from my congressman urging me to "reconsider your position", "remember those who love you", and "heed the call of duty."

It was a letter from my congressman all right, but he wasn't arguing for my coming home. He was offering me a job! It seems Bill's dad – you remember my original travelling companion – had gotten himself elected to Congress. He owned a textile company in Medellin, Colombia, which his son-in-law was running for him. He wanted me to go there and help the son-in-law out. I chuckled at the thought of what that conservative North Dallas constituency would think if they knew their congressman was offering a draft dodger a job!

I wrote back to Mr..., that is, Congressman Porter that I was not interested in accepting the job at that time as I still had some more traveling to do. This was true, but more significantly, I was terrified at the prospect of such a job. It seemed too much like a career position. I knew I would have to embark on a career someday, was even eagerly anticipating it, but not yet. There were too many things I hadn't done, too many places I hadn't seen, too many women I hadn't laid. To settle down to so much responsibility right then required more maturity than I was capable of.

But now, with my gold bars stolen and my money almost gone, I was reconsidering my position. India was no place to interrupt my travels to earn some money. There was plenty of demand for English teachers, but there were more than enough competent, English-speaking natives to meet the demand. I couldn't make it to Japan where I had originally planned on stopping on the funds I had left. Besides, I was travel weary. After two years on the road and five months since leaving Beirut, I was weary, confused, bored. Yes, bored. Not the kind of boredom that results from having nothing to do or from doing the same tedious thing day after dreary day, but the boredom that comes from a lack of direction, from not seeing any destination down life's road or any progress being made towards that destination, whatever it might be. It was tempting to accept Congressman Porter's offer and give my life some direction.

I reached the steps leading down to the Ganges, mulling all this over. The silt-laden stream flowed silently by; its reddish hue reminded me of the rivers I had known in Texas. But not much else about the scene was reminiscent of Texas. A little upstream, a shrouded corpse was being hoisted atop a funeral pyre of crisscrossed logs. The ease with which the pallbearers lifted the mortal remains indicated the poor wretch, now freed from hunger's pangs, could not have weighed more than sixty or seventy pounds at death. The mourners gathered round the pyre looked to soon be occupying the place of honor themselves. I debated whether they were weeping for the dearly departed or over their own impending fate.

At the bottom of the steps a woman was washing clothes in the muddy river, her sari tucked neatly between her legs. Just downstream from her a man was relieving himself into the murky water. Out in the middle of the stream, the fetid carcass of an emaciated cow floated by. I proceeded down the steps carefully avoiding the diarrhetic mounds of human dung which spoke to the generally poor health of the native populace and which were so common an obstacle on the sidewalks of India that we callous western youths joked about putting up signs reading "Curb Your Hindu."

While I was sitting by the river observing the human drama, a balding man in a clean saffron robe descended the steps with great dignity. In one hand he held a large umbrella; in the other, an ornate case. He stepped out onto one of the door-size wooden platforms floating in the river and moored to the bottom step. Opening his umbrella and planting it in one of the pipes attached to the platform for that purpose, he sat down cross-legged and drew from his case a variety of brightly colored creams and powders, each in its own small saucer or bowl. He placed the emollients neatly around him on the platform. In a larger bowl he floated some flower petals, jasmine perhaps. Their fragrance wafted gently up to me. Leaning forward gracefully, he scooped up some of the putrid, sanctified river water and ritualistically washed his face and arms with it. Repeating the process until he had washed his entire body, he then proceeded to beautify his body, both decoratively and aromatically, with the various creams and powders.

I don't know whether the ritual was religious or just hedonistic, but, whichever, it was an impressive display of man's ability to transcend his physical environment through his spirituality. The man was as totally immersed in the sensuality of his experience as Hugh Hefner frolicking in a hot-tub full of naked, cuddly Playmates. A look of complete serenity radiated from his face. The man was at peace, a state hard enough to attain under the best of circumstances. Attaining it amidst the filth and human degradation all around took on the proportions of a miracle.

His peace of mind became mine, as if telepathically. My problems didn't seem so significant any more. If this man could surmount the tragedy of human existence through a singleness of purpose, aided by a few aromas and adornments, I could certainly overcome the obstacles thwarting my pursuit of happiness with a little sense of purpose and a modicum of determination. The world was once again a beautiful, fascinating, challenging place.

I shouldered my backpack and started back up the steps with renewed confidence and enthusiasm. I had reached a decision. It was time to grow up, time to act responsibly. Killing gooks was not my way of proving my manhood. Nor was I fit for the martyrdom of a prison cell. I would accept Congressman Porter's offer of a job and seek my serenity in the direction and security it promised.

The cremation that was just beginning when I arrived was now over. The poor sufferer had not had sufficient funds for a large enough pyre apparently. A bony, semi-charred foot remained, to be thrown into the river along with the ashes. The sight would have disgusted me a few minutes earlier. Now it filled me with compassion. Turning full face to the river as I reached the top of the steps, I bid adieu to the Ganges.

"Thank you, Oh Holy River", I sang in silent, grateful praise.

Chapter 20 – MEDELLIN

Congressman Porter sent me an airplane ticket good for a flight from Calcutta, India to Medellin, Colombia with unlimited stopovers allowed. I stopped in Thailand, Malaysia, Singapore, Cambodia, Taiwan, Hong Kong, and Japan. But traveling by plane didn't suit my otherwise impecunious life style. The people I met on planes all had hotel reservations, important engagements, tight schedules. They never would have understood how I traveled had I mentioned it to them. Generally, I was too embarrassed to, even with the stewardesses who, if I'd revealed my sad circumstances, might have offered to share their room, if not their bed. But I never revealed my need, afraid they were more likely to shun me contemptuously as they hurried off to some fancy hotel than invite me to spend the night.

I left Japan bound for Colombia on Christmas Day, 1969. It was my third Christmas away from home. In a way it was the fourth as well, for Christmas expired before we crossed the International Date Line, then, when we did, it was Christmas Day all over again. It didn't really matter what the count was, however, as I had stopped counting.

We stopped in Vancouver and I took the opportunity to call home. It was the first time I had spoken to anyone in the family in two years. I had a remarkably normal chat with my guardian aunt, going over the doings of all the family members, including the new

112

additions – nephews, nieces, a sister-in-law. I wondered if she found it as strange as I did to be talking that way, as if I'd just been away at school for a semester or something. She refrained from making any evaluative remarks concerning my actions and made no attempt to talk me out of my chosen course. She knew how obstinate I am.

It was a clear day as we flew over the western United States on the way to Colombia. Looking down on the neatly laid out towns - the geometrically straight highways pointing the way past the grain elevator and the high school to the square where the paved arrow would be known as "Main Street", then out the other side of town past the drive-in and the filling stations to the carefully cultivated fields of grain stretching expansively to the outskirts of the next little town - made me heartrendingly nostalgic. Combined with the scenic splendor over which we flew - the volcano-capped Cascades, the sculpted canyonlands of Utah, the arid majesty of the Sonoran desert – I felt I need never leave my homeland again, if I ever got home. There was enough there of interest and beauty to fill a lifetime.

"If it weren't for Vietnam," I mused, "I'd be headed home right now. When will that damn war end!" Our engagement in Vietnam, counting just from the military buildup of 1965, had at this point lasted longer than our participation in World War II. The resolution hoped for after Nixon's election in 1968 seemed no nearer in sight. Two countries - one small, poor, embattled; the other rich, powerful, arrogant – were still being torn apart by the conflict.

I was met at the airport in Medellin by Mr. Porter's daughter, Susan, and her husband, Tom. The first test of my ability to switch from the nonchalant lifestyle of a vagabond to that of a career-minded management trainee did not go well. As was my custom at all the stops since Calcutta, I hung back while all the passengers with more urgent business pushed and shoved to get through customs. When I finally ambled through the gate, I found Susan and Tom a bit perturbed at how long they had had to wait, and rightfully so. I just wasn't used to being met at airports and hadn't been around people for whom time is money in a long time.

I didn't do much better on subsequent tests of my aptitude for metamorphosis. They say Bedouins are contemptuous of the settled people they are sometimes forced to deal with. They scoff at the dull routine of their lives, the prideful importance they attach to material symbols of status, their groveling obeisance before the clowns and fools who call themselves their rulers. To nomads, settled people are wallowing in their own shit. Well, I had the attitude of a Bedouin towards the good people of Medellin. I couldn't imagine how they tolerated the mind-numbing sameness of their life day after day. They spent the week imprisoned within four walls, talking of nothing but what fun they were going to have during their two days of semi-freedom at the end of the week. Hell, I had more interesting and exciting things happen to me every day when I was traveling than these people had in a year of weekends!

Their fear of the constricting web of social strictures under which they lived, which resulted in a conformity as featureless as their lives, I found repugnant and contemptible. This was brought dramatically home to me one day at the office when I discovered I was wearing two different shoes, one brown, one green. I found it humorous and started to laugh. When I explained what I was laughing about to my colleagues, the shocked, embarrassed looks on their faces made me realize that to them the proper behavior, were they ever to commit such a lamentable breach of etiquette, would be to discreetly withdraw and rectify the mistake, not bring it to everyone's attention.

A more telling demonstration of how out of place I was in polite society came when I befriended a couple of scruffy, twenty-something Americans who were doing Latin America much as I had done it two years earlier, only their motivation was cheap drugs more than broadening their horizon. I made the mistake of let them bunk in one of the spare bedrooms in my apartment. One day I was walking through the park they would hang out in and two uniformed officers of the law arrested me! I spent the night in the Medellin jail, packed in a communal cell with thirty or so other *desperados*, without knowing why I had been detained. In the morning, Tom sprang me. He explained that my housemates were suspected of drug-dealing and, since they lived with me, the authorities assumed I was involved. Tom was able to convince them otherwise. I could see from the incredulous look on his face that it was unfathomable to him how I could have ended up in such a mess. Not the sort of thing that befell his classmates at the Harvard Business School.

I did not shed the Bedouin mentality I had acquired from months on the road quickly, but slowly it began to wear off. Bedouin are dependent on settled people for some of the necessities of life, like pots for making tea and knives for slitting the throats of their evening meal (or other Bedouins), and I was finding the settled people had some nice things to offer me, too. As a settled person, I was living much more comfortably than I had on the road. Some of the creature comforts, such as the extra two bedrooms in my three-story apartment, I could do without; but some, like my motorcycle, I was becoming quite fond of.

"Now let's see, what shall I do on the weekend?" I was soon asking myself.

Had I been truly career oriented, as I thought I was ready to be when I took the job, I would have appreciated more what a tremendous opportunity I had fallen into. It was clear that I had been hired to take over the managing of the textile company in a year or two so that Tom and Susan, having had their Junior Year Abroad fling, could return to more cosmopolitan pursuits in the United States. Being the manager of an American-owned company in a foreign country was about my idea of a perfect position. Though it might not pay as well as a stateside job, it would provide me with more luxury than I knew how to enjoy. Medellin - not known then, as it was a decade later, for its drug cartels - was a charming, bustling city nestled in a beautiful valley midst tropical splendor and blessed with an equable climate thanks to its five-thousand-foot elevation. I loved living abroad and I loved Latin America. I had it made!

Only I didn't fit in. Tom and Susan I got along with fine. Susan I knew almost as well as I knew her brother Bill. She was a really nice person, and Tom seemed decent, too. But the position they occupied in Colombian society I considered not so nice. On fire with Marxist/Leninist anti-imperialist indignation, I looked on them - abstractly, not personally - as capitalist exploiters, draining the wealth from a poor, underdeveloped country while subverting the local government to protect their holdings by any means necessary from the revolutionary rage of the impoverished masses. If the guerrillas, who were forever and everywhere in countries like Colombia lurking in the hills, should ever succeed in marching on the capital, frightened gringos like Tom and Susan would be screaming for our government to send in the Marines. I suspected I would be cheering the guerrillas on. (Some years later, when Tom and Susan learned they were on the kidnap-for-ransom list of my heroic guerrillas, they grabbed up the kids and hurriedly returned to the United States.)

I didn't care much for Tom's and Susan's collaborators, either: the corrupt oligarchy which had ruled the country since Spanish times. Their interests – economic and social - were so tied to foreign capital as to make their perspective on their fellow citizens almost indistinguishable from that of their American business partners. Behind high walls, topped with broken glass, they lived a life of luxury as divorced from that of the average Colombian as was our 19th century robber barons' from that of the huddled masses washing up on our shores tired and poor. Yet, personally these elitist scumbags struck me as warm, decent, generous people. Funny!

There was one Colombian banker I met, for instance, who had a broader, more patriotic understanding of his country's plight.

"What do you think the prospects for my country's future are?" the banker asked as we sipped cocktails at an evening soiree.

From what I learned about the Third World in my two years travelling around it, I thought it was pretty bleak.

"Bright," I responded, trying to be polite. Most Colombian bankers I'd met exuded an unbridled optimism when it came to the future (while they tucked their money away in Swiss bank accounts just in case they were wrong).

"I wish I shared your opinion," the banker went on. "But I'm afraid things are likely to get worse."

"You don't think you're in the take-off stage?" I asked, starting to think this conversation might be more interesting than I had expected.

I had used a buzzword on the lips of every World Bank and USAID official at the time, taken from a book called *The Stages of Economic Growth* by an economic historian named Walt Rostow. The subtitle of the book, *A Non-Communist Manifesto*, made clear where Rostow was coming from, as did his understanding of the stages a country must go through to achieve the "Age of Mass Consumption", as Rostow labelled that final stage of growth where the people of even the most forlorn country would be living like Americans.

The book was sophomoric drivel. It was a simplistic restatement of the stages countries like ours had gone through in achieving our elevated level of mass prosperity. To apply it to Third World countries that had missed out on being in the forefront of the Industrial Revolution was ludicrous. For instance, Rostow argued for free trade, i.e., low tariff barriers, while our own industries had depended on high tariffs to attain the "take-off stage" in the 19th century. Rostow postulated that growth is initially stimulated by the export of raw materials - exactly the role the colonies play in the classic imperialist setup. By this logic, Chile would advance to the take-off stage by exporting more and more of its copper to the motherland, i.e. us, which is what we were counting on as our own mines petered out. This self-serving pablum was doled out at conference after conference dedicated to resolving the disparity in living standards between the prosperous, industrialized countries and the rest of the world. (Rostow saw China and India as having achieved take off in 1952 – off by thirty years in China's case; India is still waiting.)

"I don't put much faith in Mr. Rostow's stages of economic growth," the banker said, his words music to my skeptical ears. "What worked for you is not likely to work for us. For one thing we don't have the market; we are not a continent-sized country like America. Moreover, while America depended on massive foreign investment to develop its resources, making the British rich, its economy was big enough to absorb it, so that by the beginning of the 20th century the United States had become productive enough to switch from being a debtor nation to a creditor nation."

"But can't Colombia do the same?" I argued, playing the Devil's Advocate. "You've got oil resources that need foreign capital to be exploited. In the end, that investment will yielded dividends many time over for Colombians."

"And for the foreign investors," the banker countered. "You have to understand that foreign capitalists invest in Colombia with the expectation of making a profit, and they expect to be able to repatriate those profits abroad. That's different than if Colombians invested their own capital and the profits remained in this country to finance additional growth. That's why we have to put stringent controls on the remittance of profits abroad." (When Tom and Susan fled the country, they repatriated the proceeds from the sale of Mr. Porter's company in their luggage!)

"Which doesn't work all that well since your banker friends want to get their money out of the country, too, in preparation for a rainy day." Now I was revealing my Marxist leanings. I might as well have been quoting Lenin's *Imperialism, The Highest Stage of Capitalism*.

"Quite right. You seem to understand some of the problems we face," the banker concluded, before heading off to get another drink.

(Bromides like *The Stages of Economic Growth* are still being offered up by the World Bank, fraudulently holding out hope to the poor and desperate that prosperity is just around the corner, if they will but follow the sage advice of their betters, who do very well if the suckers do follow their advice. The current slogan is "Ending Extreme Poverty by 2030". How? More of the same.)

The conversation with the sober-minded Colombian banker was atypical. Most conversations of that nature I had with the class of Colombians I would be socializing with if I remained at Mr. Porter's textile company ended in contempt - often mutual. But it wasn't dislike for the role I saw myself destined to play that caused me to decide to forsake my golden career opportunity and leave Colombia. It was a more immediate, mundane concern, plus a more personal one. My passport would expire in less than a year. It was hard to contemplate long-term career plans with that prospect in so near a future. Then there was Samira. I was still infatuated, still wondered if she was the woman with whom I wanted to share the rest of my life. I'd hardly been in touch with her over the last year - a couple of letters back and forth several months apart. I wasn't much of a letter writer and her letters came tardily by way of my home in Dallas since that was the only sure address I could give her. She had said she would wait for me, but could I really expect her to? It would take a tremendous act of faith on her part to believe she was ever going to see me again. And she wasn't get any younger. By Arab standards she was, at 25, almost over the hill - just one more refused proposal from a cousin away from lifelong spinsterhood.

On the other hand, if she was waiting, what an awesome responsibility that put on me! Such a commitment could not just be ignored, as I had ignored other responsibilities like military service. I was still plagued with guilt over that first girl, the joy of my Summer of Love, who had had her dream turned into a nightmare because of my self-serving, self-gratifying lying. I didn't want to be responsible for another life turned bitter because of me, especially not the life of one so trusting, so vulnerable, and so loving as Samira. I would have to put an end to her waiting - if she was waiting - either by telling her it was futile or by returning to her.

So, after six months in Colombia, I departed Medellin and set off to return to Beirut. The Lebanese government, with its *laissez faire* attitude toward things in general and political refugees in particular, seemed more likely to shrug their shoulders and look the other way when my passport expired than the U.S.-beholden Colombian government. My second exposure to corporate living - the first having been at the Stanford Business School - convinced me I wanted to do something else with my life than make money, perhaps pursue an academic career. The American University of Beirut might not be as renowned academically as the institutions I had attended previously, but it was a good school and in subjects related to the Middle East on a par with the best. I would pursue a Master's degree there while waiting for that infernal war in Southeast Asia to come to an end.

Chapter 21 – BEIRUT BOUND

Looking back, I can't believe how casually I decided to pick up roots and travel half way round the world on the basis of some shaky political speculations, a fuzzy career plan, and the sweet but vague recollection of a girl I barely knew. And with only a couple of hundred dollars with which to do it! I made the decision as nonchalantly as if I was moving from Dallas to Fort Worth. Ah, the reckless, unbounded self-confidence of youth!

The first leg of the trip was traveling down the Amazon by boat, then to Rio by bus. I was passing by Rio in hopes of finding a cheap way back across the Atlantic, like working on a freighter (My father had gotten to Japan that way when he was about my age). I also hoped to see some old friends, which I did. Bob had lost his job for reasons he cared not to relate and was living his alternative lifestyle more openly now, comfortably cohabiting with a "tall and tan and young and lovely" boy from Ipanema. He seemed happy. Steve was still up in the Amazon hunting for diamonds... or insurgents.

Marie Ines was barely recognizable. She had shed the combat gear for the fashionable attire of your typical Avenida Copacabana promenader. She looked good - more of a woman, less of a girl - though I still only looked on her as an intellectual sparring partner. Her change of attire reflected a change in her political perspective. Instead of the sayings of Mao Tse-tung, she now quoted Roberto

Campos, the Brazilian Minister of the Economy whose thinking was so in tune with that of his American advisors that Brazilians called him "Bob Fields," a direct translation of his name. In the same patronizing way she once instructed me in dialectical materialism, she now lectured me on what a fool I was for not doing my military service. She urged me to go home. I felt betrayed, unsure of myself. In the two years since we had seen each other, I had become as radicalized, as anti-imperialist, which implied anti-American, as she had been transformed into a mouthpiece for the status quo. In the end I concluded she was the one who had metamorphosed in the wrong direction, not me.

Passage across the Atlantic as a hand on a freighter didn't work out (My father had done it, but that was in 1927, when the Seaman's Union wasn't so strong). Instead I flew to Dakar, Senegal with the intent to see a little of West Africa before crossing the Sahara to Tunisia and heading east to Beirut from there. That's pretty much how it worked out.

I toured West Africa in my usual impecunious style - dodging cholera outbreaks - then hitched a ride across the Sahara from Agades, Niger to Tamanrasset, Algeria with some Libyan sheep smugglers. Actually, I was a paying passenger, along with six other itinerants: an American also embarked on the Grand Tour, some Liberians emigrating to Europe, and a couple of French university students heading home. For ten dollars, we got to ride in the back of the truck, crammed in with a hundred or so sharp-hooved, constantly bleating sheep. There were three trucks and a station wagon in our convoy. We had to delay our departure three days because it was the end of the rainy season and the smugglers were afraid of getting stuck in the mud. Stuck in the mud... in the Sahara Desert!

I call our chauffeurs smugglers because when they left the confines of Agades there were only a dozen or so sheep in the three trucks; once past the customs post on the edge of town, they loaded another couple of hundred sheep, hidden in a *wadi* (dry river bed), onto the trucks. I'm sure the Libyans and the Nigerois border police - who couldn't possibly have fallen for such a transparent ruse - considered it just a shrewd business practice, but I'm equally sure frustrated bureaucrats back in the capital trying to introduce modern methods in an economy still based on the camel would have called it smuggling. In honor of their noble but futile efforts, so do I.

They were an aloof lot, the smugglers. They barely deigned to speak to us passengers, contemptuous of us either as infidels or because, despite hailing from the affluent West, we were so poor we had to cross the Sahara in the back of a truck. As to the sheep, every once in a while particularly loud and pathos-filled bleating signaled one of their kind had died from the overcrowding and the smugglers would stop and toss the dearly departed unceremoniously off the truck. I had a feeling that if one of their two-legged cargo succumbed to the choking dust kicked up by vehicles or the burning desert heat, they would have just as matter of factly disposed of the human carcass in that way.

But, with Samira on my mind, I was in a mood to romanticize Arabs, so when the smugglers ran down a fleeing gazelle with the station wagon for their evening meal and rubbed its body with water before slitting its throat, I interpreted the water massage as an act of compassion prescribed by their Islamic faith, like the kosher ritualized slaughter of animals. My more cynical American companion, unmoved by any affection for Arabs - singular or plural - pointed out that washing the animal relaxed the muscles and thus tenderized the meat. My romanticism was further dampened that evening when my beloved Arabs cooked up the succulent meat and didn't offer any of us so much as a bite!

I made it across the Sahara - without ever tasting of gazelle - and arrived in Tunis a month or so after leaving Brazil. There I stayed with a college friend who was now serving in the Peace Corps. I was more than a little envious. He was "fulfilling his military obligation" the intelligent way. An undergraduate degree had been followed by a deferred year abroad on a Fulbright scholarship, then two years of deferment while he got his MBA from Harvard. Now as a Peace Corps volunteer, he had graciously been deferred again by his draft board. Then, halfway through his Peace Corps service, they instituted the draft lottery, whereby a number from 1 to 366 was assigned by drawing to each day in the year. The number determined the precedence in which draftees would be ordered to report for induction, based on their birthday. My friend's birthday came up number 363. Assured of not being drafted, he cut short his Peace Corps stint and returned to the United States to embark on a lucrative career in corporate America. Why couldn't I be that intelligent, and lucky?

I knew I would be passing through Tunis when I left Brazil so I had given my friend's address as my next mail stop. There were several letters waiting for me there, including a two-hundred-dollar investment in my future I had asked my aunt for. For some reason she had acquiesced without a murmur; maybe she liked not having me around. Less heartwarming was the news that a second brother had dropped out of Dartmouth and was now a medic in Vietnam. Also forwarded was a Hallmark-type card with a lovely sunset on the front and a message inside written in a child-like scrawl. I didn't recognize the handwriting until I glanced down to the valediction and made out the name "Samira." It was a love letter. She was writing it, I read, on the day of her graduation from the American University of Beirut three months previous. She was still in her white graduation dress, seated on the bench - "our bench" - where we had sat and chatted and watched the sun set over the Mediterranean after our day at the races.

"I'm very lonely," she wrote, "There was no one here to see me graduate – no family, no friends, and worst of all, no Ken. Do you remember me, the little village girl whose heart you stole? No, you didn't steal it; I gave it to you gladly. And I don't want it back. I'm going home to Beit Jala now. I have a job teaching in Bethlehem. I'll be living with my mother, gossiping with her about goings-on in the village, but my mind will be elsewhere, dreaming of my tall, handsome American somewhere out there in the world beyond the sea. Will I ever see him again? If I do, he'll find me waiting for him. I love him still."

There were tears wetting my cheeks as I finished the letter. "She *was* waiting for me!" I exulted. At least that part of my plan was not total foolishness. Of course, she wouldn't be in Beirut when I got there, a contingency which should have occurred to me before I set out to travel 10,000 miles to be with her but hadn't. But that's all right. I would get myself established - get a job, find a place for us to live; then I'd figure out some way to get her back to Beirut.

I floated along the northern side of the Mediterranean from Tunis to Beirut as if on angel's wings (in reality, on one slow ferry after another). In Athens I shared a room with an American chick, attractive enough. Everything in my experience told me she was willing, but I didn't even try.

"This must be love!" I marveled.

Chapter 22 – THE MARCH

A week after landing back in Beirut I found a job at the American Community School, replacing a teacher who had been caught in a dalliance with a student and summarily shipped back home. ACS was a prep school which catered to American families living all over the Middle East. The teaching position entitled me to a room at the school as well. My masterful plan, so carefully thought out, was working to perfection. Then I read a tidbit in the local English-language paper which was to put a kink in my plan.

What I read was that Congress was considering authorizing $500 million for Israel in the 1970 foreign aid bill. This marked the first time we would be providing direct aid to the Zionist state on such a large scale. Private individuals had contributed hundreds of millions of dollars through the United Jewish Appeal and similar organizations, but the government had kept its support diplomatic or covert, bowing to the sensitivities of the Arabs about the pariah in their midst. This new allotment I considered a major escalation in our support for the Zionist State. Something had to be done about it.

With this in mind I went to see Jack Henderson, an American I'd worked for my first stint in Beirut. I knew he was involved with a group of resident Americans who published a newsletter on the Arab-Israeli conflict dedicated to opening the eyes of the folks back home. The group was called "Americans for Justice in the Middle East" (AJME). Jack was chatting with an American graduate student

I knew, Brian Thompson. I mentioned my concern about the proposed funds for Israel and, half jestingly, suggested we march on the embassy in protest (It was the 60's; peaceably assembling was in vogue). I was taken aback by the enthusiasm with which both Jack and Brian greeted the idea.

"I can get 150 people out from AJME," Jack promised.

"And I can get that many students from the university," Brian chimed in.

With that, the wobbly egg I had hatched began to roll. We picked Thanksgiving Day, four days away, for the march. Jack and Brian would spread the word and we would have an organizing meeting the next night at Jack's place. I was to try and find out what sort of permission we might need from the Lebanese government to march the half mile down the seaside corniche from AUB's lower gate to the American embassy.

I thought the president of AUB's student council might be able to give me some guidance on how to obtain a permit for the march as he and his cohorts frequently utilized the paved soapbox. I tracked him down the next evening on the steps of the university's assembly hall. He was waiting to welcome the Lebanese Prime Minister, Saeb Salam, who was to speak to the students.

"Why don't you ask the Prime Minister himself," the president suggested when I explained to him what I wanted.

It seemed presumptuous to bother a prime minister over such a trifling matter, but I also realized it would be presumptuous of me to assume I knew proper etiquette in someone else's country. So I went to the reception following the speech and, after being introduced to Mr. Salam by the student council president, humbly put my question to him.

"Of course you can march!" the Prime Minister said ebulliently. "You have my personal permission."

Mr. Salam, a roly-poly man with an avuncular manner but piercing eyes that suggested you didn't want to mess with him, reminded me of the merchants in the souk.

"And I'll see that you are properly escorted," he went on, as if offering me a special deal because I was his friend. "But Americans only," he instructed the students, with a wave of his ever present cigar past the trademark carnation in his lapel.

I was elated and rushed over to Jack's to tell the meeting I was already late to the good news. The five or six people there were excited to hear we'd been sanctioned at such a high level, everyone that is except Brian who seemed more disconcerted than thrilled by the news. He excused himself shortly thereafter. We drew up a petition on which we were all to get signatures and scheduled a final, poster-making meeting for the following night.

The next morning the front page of Beirut's English-language daily, *The Daily Star*, featured a bold-faced box proclaiming "JOIN THE 1000 AMERICANS MARCHING ON THE U.S. EMBASSY THANKSGIVING DAY." At first I thought some other group must be planning a march; we had no such grandiose expectations. But I soon learned Jack had placed the ad on his own initiative and with his own money. I appreciated the effort but thought it might be counter-productive.

Other Americans had a less than positive reaction. The American embassy started calling around to American companies advising them to discourage their American employees from participating, an infringement of their constitutional rights which would have brought the wrath of the ACLU down upon them had it taken place in the States. The AUB administration sent a memo around to their staff saying the march had not been approved by the Lebanese government. This particularly annoyed me as the dean who signed the memo had been at the reception where the Prime Minister had given his wholehearted endorsement. (Years later, this same dean would be gunned down in his office by a crazed Palestinian, who had perhaps caught him in an equally egregious fib.)

I ran into Jack later that morning. Always one to react in extremes, his extreme enthusiasm of two days back was now superseded by an extreme agitation.

"We've got to call off the march!" he shrieked. "Everyone's going berserk! The embassy thinks the PFLP (Popular Front for the Liberation of Palestine) is behind it. Someone's got to go talk to them and calm them down, explain to them that it's an entirely American event, and completely non-violent."

I was sort of pleased that the embassy was getting upset, but Jack convinced me it would be a good thing to talk with them. Somehow he got me to agree to be the one to do it (I had studiously avoided walking into any American embassy since leaving Beirut a year earlier). The egg I hatched was becoming a snowball growing in size as it rolled down the hill right at me.

I called up the embassy and arranged a meeting with the Deputy Chief of Mission, a Mr. Hilton. He received me cordially and we were having a friendly chat - Ivy Leaguer to Ivy Leaguer - when he received a phone call. Someone deep within the bowels of the embassy informed him that there was a warrant out for my arrest.

"Are you sure? I can't believe it," Mr. Hilton kept repeating, unable to believe that this personable young man before him could be wanted by the law.

Either because the person on the other end of the phone was shouting or because Mr. Hilton's head was hollow, I could hear the whole conversation. Wanting to get it over with and spare Mr. Hilton further embarrassment, I shouted out "It's me! It's me already!"

"Send the consul up, please," Mr. Hilton said tonelessly into the phone.

The consul, a Mr. Morris, was a fastidious type in appearance and manner. His cool demeanor towards me made it clear he didn't care for me on principle. He read out loud the State Department communique informing Beirut that my passport had been revoked.

"I'm afraid I'll have to ask you for your passport, Mr. Kiask," he announced, with a quirky smile which told me he was enjoying this. (Years later, when I had obtained my files from the State Department under the Freedom of Information Act, I would read his formulaic assessment of me: "mentally unbalanced, possibly capable of violence.")

Stupidly, I had brought my passport to the embassy with me. I thought I would need it to get past the guards. I toyed with the idea of refusing to hand it over but assumed the consul would just invite a couple of Marines up to beat it out of me if I did. I surrendered my passport. Then, to my surprise, the two men ushered me to the embassy door and bid me "Good day." I expected to be arrested on the spot.

Walking back to the American Community School along the corniche we were to march down the next day, I felt the same sense of relief I had felt on that train platform in Turkey. My flight was over, the future ordained. The Moving Finger had written once again, and His pencil had no eraser. I resolved to pursue the march with renewed vigor, then await my fate. I decided not to mention the loss of my passport to anyone.

"What's this I hear about you losing your passport?" asked one of the teachers at ACS as we met on our way into dinner later that day.

"How did he know?" I wondered.

At dinner it became apparent the embassy had contacted the school about the march when the headmaster announced that any student participating in it would be suspended. Evidently, discovering a draft dodger was behind the march was no more reassuring to the embassy than their original supposition of the PFLP being behind it. Several teachers at the school who had promised to participate now remembered prior commitments.

The pre-march meeting at Jack's apartment that night did nothing to lift my spirits. The enthusiasm of the half dozen people there was repeatedly dampened by Jack's hysterical ranting that the whole thing was a big mistake and should be called off. I argued that it was too late for that, especially after Jack had publicly committed us with that ad. I carried the day, or thought I did. Jack promised to bring the posters we had made to the starting point of the march the next afternoon.

Thanksgiving Day dawned gray and bleary, perfectly matching my mood. I felt I was about to preside over a fiasco. That rolling ball I had nudged along was now a tumbling boulder threatening to crush me. Unenthusiastically, I went through the motions: collecting petitions, borrowing a bullhorn, encouraging people to turn out. I arrived at the starting point outside AUB's lower gate fifteen minutes early. What I saw there did nothing to lift my spirits.

A platoon of M-16 toting Red Berets, Lebanon's special security force, were lounging about leaning against the wall that lined the corniche. Saeb Salam had kept his promise to protect us. From what I wasn't sure. Or whether there would be anyone to protect. The only Americans in evidence were news crews from the TV networks: ABC, NBC, CBS. They, along with their Lebanese counterparts, had turned out in force, at least. The soldiers and the newsmen looked at me, bullhorn and petitions in hand, with an accusatory glare as they stood there in the intermittent rain. I noticed the rain was washing the signatures off the petitions.

"Oh well," I consoled myself, "They're mostly the signatures of ACS kids too young to vote anyway."

At three o'clock, the hour set for the march, I stood there alone - the entire march contingent. Even Jack hadn't shown up with the posters.

"My humiliation is complete," I thought.

I was raising the bullhorn to my mouth to announce the cancellation of the march, when a crowd - obviously Americans - began pouring out of the AUB gate. My enthusiasm and confidence restored, I began instructing them with the bullhorn where to form up. Nobody paid me the slightest attention. When I saw Mr. Hilton and Mr. Morris amongst the umbrella-toting throng, bemused smiles on their faces, it dawned on me that this was the crowd from the annual ACS Thanksgiving Day football game, held on the AUB campus.

"*Now* my humiliation is complete!" I moaned.

Once again I prepared to announce the cancellation of the march. As I groped for some face-saving words that might avert the soldiers turning their rifles on me or the newsmen their sarcasm, a bunch of rag-tag American students from the university came out the gate right behind the football fans. I recognized some of them as part of the politically active segment of the American contingent at AUB. Their leader came up and told me the group had considered the march too pacific for their taste, but when they heard the embassy was trying to squelch it they decided it merited their support.

All in all, we ended up with about a hundred marchers. We moved down the corniche between two columns of Red Berets, newsmen darting in and out for sound bites. Our posters read "USA, not UJA", "Give thanks, not tanks" and things like that, Jack having finally shown up about the same time as the students. We were a merry little band. Everyone was having a good time being interviewed and photographed, so the absurdity of delivering a petition to the embassy on a day when it was closed didn't occur to anyone. Nor did they laugh at the pathetic polemic I delivered when we reached our destination, my incoherent rambling mercifully drowned out by the hoots and jeers the students directed at a dark figure on the embassy roof taking pictures.

The march was judged a success when the Arab newspapers came out the next morning with photos of the march prominently displayed. We even heard a snippet of the march had gotten on the evening news back in the States. Only two things marred the completeness of our victory. One was that, despite the outcry from its far-flung colony, the U.S. Congress overwhelmingly approved the authorization of the half billion dollars for Israel. The other only affected me personally: the loss of my passport.

Chapter 23 – LIMBO

"And where will you be working next week?" the head of the math department at ACS asked smugly a few days after the march. That was my official notification that the offer I had received the previous week of extending my job at ACS until the end of the year had been rescinded. No matter. I'd find another. I had a more pressing concern at the moment anyway: how could I arrange to stay in Lebanon without a passport?

Having no idea of the proper protocol in such matters and having enjoyed such success by going right to the top in the matter of the march, I decided I would try that approach again. I drafted a most respectful letter, addressed to the Prime Minister, in which I requested permission to remain in Lebanon. Saeb Salam's personal secretary, into whose hands I entrusted the letter, was a Levantine of such classic unctuousness he might as well have let the letter slip from his greasy hands into the waste basket before my very eyes, despite his assurances he would see that the Prime Minister received it immediately. Undaunted, I returned to the Prime Minister's office several times to see if anything had come of my letter. On the fourth trip the secretary informed me everything had been taken care of and I should go to the *Sureté Nationale*, Lebanon's equivalent of the FBI, to formalize things. From his brusque manner, I could see he hoped that would be the last he would see of me.

I went to the *Sureté* but couldn't find anyone aware of the Prime Minister having given any attention to my case. The official I was being interviewed by pretended not to understand when I explained I had no passport, no visa, despite his having conversed in excellent English up to that point. Finding me slow on the uptake, the harried official finally blurted out "Get out!" - not out of the country; just out of his office. It dawned on me I constituted a nuisance nobody wanted to bother with. I concluded I could stay in Lebanon sans passport and sans visa indefinitely, so long as I didn't cause any trouble.

And so I entered a state of limbo. Jack gave me a job teaching English. I rented the apartment of the teacher I'd replaced at ACS. I applied to the history department at the university to enter the Master's program. Amazingly, the loss of my passport hadn't really affected my plans except for one thing: I couldn't go see Samira. My original plan when I formulated it in Medellin was to establish myself in Beirut, then invite Samira to come and shack up with me, i.e. cohabitate. That was the standard courtship ritual of the time: get to know one another before you commit to each other for life (Good theory; didn't really work out that well in practice). In retrospect, I find it hard to believe I was so ignorant of Arab mores. If Samira had tried to take me up on my invitation, she wouldn't have made it to Beirut alive. A frank exchange with Samira, through letters, provided insight into Arab courtship rituals. They didn't include shacking up. In fact, they usually didn't include any moments alone for the lovebirds prior to the wedding.

In the absence of a father, Samira's oldest brother, an officer in King Hussein's intelligence service, was the supreme arbiter on matters concerning the family. The mother didn't count for squat. The brother would not entertain any notion of Samira and me even seeing each other. Even if I proposed marriage – and I wasn't about to do that; I hardly knew the girl! – he would have nixed the idea out of hand; she had plenty of eligible cousins to choose from. So, though she pined for me still, Samira would not be coming to Beirut and I could not go to Palestine. My love life, like my legal status, was in limbo.

If only that damn war would come to an end! Perhaps in the spirit of "binding up the nation's wounds" there would follow some forgiveness for people like me. Public opinion was turning more and more against the war. Even former Attorney General Ramsey Clark, was speaking out against it. War resisters were increasingly being seen as justified; to some, even heroic. But reconciliation could only come after the war was over, and the war showed no signs of resolving itself in either victory or defeat. Nixon had just upped the ante by secretly invading Cambodia; American troop strength in Vietnam remained constant at around a half million men; the body bags continued to pile up on runways in Hawaii, while the "body count", the army's official tally of Vietcong killed, assumed astronomical proportions. The end was nowhere in sight.

And so the years dragged by. I started work on a Masters degree in Arab History at AUB. They gave me a graduate assistantship, which, along with teaching part-time at Jack's language school, covered my room and board. I wrote Samira occasionally, and she wrote me back. At some point - I can't remember how or when - I proposed to her by mail, that being the only way we could be together, it seemed. She accepted by return post. It seemed crazy, marrying a girl I had known for a month and from a culture radically different from my own, but I felt I knew one thing about her which I trusted would see us through any post-wedding surprises: she has a good heart. Not that our pledges of matrimony affected our geographic separation one iota.

To say the years "dragged by" is not exactly accurate. Beirut was a wonderful place to be in the early 70's. The Lebanese flair for living trickled down to all levels of society, making for a comfortable, pleasant existence even for one living a life of imposed frugality like me. Blue jeans were available cheaper than you could buy them in the United States; opulent, gold-leafed movie theaters offered first-run American movies at a third of the price back home; the best imported liquors, as well as passable local imitations, could be had at cut-rate prices (I never drank as well - before or since - as during those impoverished, graduate-student days in Beirut!). We even had an A & P, though the perfectly replicated (and trademark infringing!) logo on the storefront stood for Antoine & Pierre, not the Great Atlantic and Pacific Tea Company.

It was an exciting place to be, too. My teaching duties were periodically interrupted by student strikes protesting one political development or another; the Palestinians were gaining strength in the refugee camps, provoking occasional strafing of the camps by both the Israelis and the Lebanese; the whole Arab world, reflected in microcosm in Beirut by ubiquitous spies, secretly funded newspapers, and secretly armed factions, was in a state of turmoil as it struggled to come to grips with the shock of its defeat at the hands of the Israelis. For an intrigued observer whose political awareness had been stimulated by a different conflict faraway, it was heady stuff.

So let's just say the years glided by - way too many of them, for me and for our country. Like me, the country was stuck in limbo as it stumbled – dazed and confused - through the longest war in our history. My inability to see any way out of my personal dilemma was mirrored by those in power, who couldn't seem to see a way out of our national morass. The war just went on and on, year after year.

Chapter 24 – SPOOKS

Let me introduce Jack Henderson, erstwhile march co-organizer and proprietor of the American Language Center where I taught part-time, as he is symbolic of a whole new world which opened up to me during my years in Beirut. A handsome, intelligent, personable fellow in his early forties, the son of a general in the U.S. Army, Jack had come to the Middle East in the mid-1960's to teach at the Aleppo American College in Syria. When that institution was closed down by a suspicious Syrian government in the wake of the 1967 war, he had been given the American Language Center by the United States Information Agency (USIA), which was anxious to sever its ties (at least the overt ones) to the Center.

Now, if you put all that together, you might come to the same conclusion a lot of people did: that Jack was a spy. You should understand it didn't take much to earn that honorific in Beirut; I myself was so honored by a number of people, especially the radical student element at AUB. Beirut abounded in spies: Cold War spies, Israeli spies, spies representing every member of the Arab League, free-lancing spies who answered to no one but the dollar. The spies masqueraded as newsmen, teachers, missionaries, businessmen, diplomats – and, perhaps, as the director of a language school. It was said that if Lebanon ever cleansed itself of spies, half the bars in Beirut would go bankrupt. It was the fake moustache capital of the world!

I never did decide about Jack myself, still haven't. He certainly worked at cultivating the myth of being a clandestine operative, if myth it was. When he went on one of his frequent trips back home, he didn't announce his plans in advance or say when he'd be back. He would just be gone one day. A week or two later he would reappear. He would turn up in bizarre places - like amongst the student volunteers on work trips to the refugee camps - where he stood out like a stripper at a convent. It was he, it should be remembered, who finagled me into going to the embassy and consequently losing my passport. After that loss, he proposed arranging for me to be spirited into Palestine, aka Israel, to be with my true love. It wasn't clear whether I was to be escorted across the border by Palestinian guerrillas on their way to raid a kibbutz or compatriots of mine associated with a secretive agency whose name begins with "C". It was just the sort of weird thing Jack would suggest, the sort of thing which made people wonder about him.

Less difficult to fathom were the Americans enrolled in AUB's Middle East Area Studies program, a graduate program set up by the U.S. Army in the early fifties to train its intelligence officers. It had since dropped its army affiliation but was generally assumed to be still fulfilling the same function. The healthy, gung-ho, clean-cut young men enrolled in the program, who apparently had no difficulties with their draft boards, did little to dispel the notion.

One of the students enrolled in the program was Brian Thompson, the guy who had once promised to get out 150 students for the march, then disappeared from sight. Well, almost disappeared. Looking over the photos in the Lebanese papers the day after the march, I was surprised to see Brian there amongst the demonstrators. Surprised because he had faded out of sight so quickly a few days earlier and because, on that dark and dismal day, he was wearing sunglasses.

I mentioned this jokingly to the student sitting next to me in the AUB milk bar where I was perusing the paper.

"Oh, yeah. That's typical. He's known around here as the 'CIA Student in Residence'," he informed me. "He's really a spooky guy. A friend of mine credits that bastard with getting her busted for drugs when she went back to the States.

A quintessential straight-arrow WASP, Brian was known around campus for his persistent nosiness and malicious rumor-mongering. With his habit of peppering his conversation with disparaging remarks about "niggers" and "Hebes", he was not a likable guy. Yet, perversely, he and I got along fine. I think I must be a hard-rock conservative deep down, thrust into a radical role by untoward circumstances, for I often prefer the company of conservatives to that of liberals. In a grossly generalizing sort of way, I find conservatives ignorant but honest; liberals, world-wise but sleazy, and I figure it's easier to educate an ignorant person than to make a dishonest person honest.

One evening, a month or so after the march, I ran into Brian as I walked home from the university. He was in a foul mood, having just driven down from the Lebanese ski resort of Faraya on his motorcycle in a freezing rain because the American students he hoped to stay with had refused to let him spend the night. He invited me over to his place for a drink, which surprised me as he had refused to tell me where he lived up till then.

We had a glass of wine, then Brian got out some hashish, which also came as a surprise as I had considered him too straight to indulge. "Maybe the United States has changed more than I know in the three years I've been gone," I thought. Normally, I partook when marijuana went around, just to be sociable, not because I really enjoyed it. Like a contemporary who famously confessed during his successful run for the Presidency to having tried weed, I didn't inhale. I wondered if Brian was trying to set me up, so this time I abstained.

"Why don't you go down to the embassy and see if you can't make a deal with them," Brian suggested as talk turned to my legal status.

"What sort of deal could I make with them?" I asked, skeptical but inquisitive.

"Well, you might work out some mutually acceptable arrangement. You know there are other ways to serve your country than going to Vietnam."

"Such as," I asked, still curious.

"You could be useful to them right here in Lebanon. You created a lot of goodwill with the Arabs with that march. Hell, the Prime Minister even knows who you are!" he said, taking a toke on the joint.

Whether Brian was following a script or the pot had loosened his tongue, I couldn't say. I wondered if this was an official offer of employment, but scoffed at the idea that anyone would entrust Brian with such a task. In any case, I changed the subject without letting Brian know I had no intention of following up on his suggestion.

Brian raised the idea of striking a deal every time I saw him after that. Then, in an about-face, just before I was scheduled to attend a hearing at the embassy on the revocation of my passport, both Brian and Jack warned me not to set foot in the embassy. Now I started to get paranoid. I wondered whether I wasn't a ball being kicked around by competing factions within the embassy – State Department versus CIA. I didn't like it and considered it unfair. So I called up Consul Morris to express my objection.

"I'll check this out with the ambassador right away," Morris assured me in his smug manner. The next day he called me back and informed me, enigmatically, "Neither Mr. Henderson nor Mr. Thompson are presently employed by the United States Government."

I was as much in the dark as ever. Were Jack and Brian warning me out of a sincere concern for my welfare or were they just performing an official duty? Which raised the question whether their friendship was genuine or professional. Whatever the case, I attended the hearing at the embassy. Nothing much came of it, except Morris' snooty promise I could get a passport good only for direct travel to the United States anytime I wanted it.

It's a troubling thing to be befriended by someone with ulterior motives. It destroys your faith in human decency; makes you hard, vengeful. Through my dealings over the years with Jack, Brian, and others like them, I came to understand how a seduced and deceived lover feels. But no matter how devastating it is to be deceived, it must be equally ruinous to be the deceiver (my own deception during the "Summer of Love" had convinced me of that). The impact on the psyche of a spy from living a life of pretense, deception, lies, has got to be demoralizing, literally.

"All the world's a stage", but for the most part we restrict our play-acting to reasonably innocuous plotting: corporate brown-nosing to land a promotion, misleading claims to sell a car, honey-coated whisperings to get laid. To be engaged professionally in constant deceit, especially when it can be a matter of life and death, boggles my mind. How could it not pervert the soul? As with cat-chomping Navy Seals, I wondered who deprograms these misanthropes so they can live amongst their simple, straightforward neighbors when their service is over. Can they transition to being decent, neighborly types, or do they plot PTA coups over backyard barbecues? No wonder governments hesitate to create super-secret entities and often come to regret it if they do.

Yet the life of a spy has its appeal - witness all the spy novels on the bestsellers list. One person who had succumbed to the appeal was my Canadian roommate in Beirut, Ian. Ian's father had been the Canadian military attaché in Jordan when Ian was young. Ian's grandfather was the general in charge of Canadian intelligence after World War I who came up with Defence Plan A, "A Plan for the Defence of Canada", the cornerstone of which was a surprise attack *on the United States* (who else is likely to attack Canada?). The idea was that this tactic would delay our invasion long enough for the British to come to Canada's rescue! With that sort of ancestry, how could Ian not be deeply into the political intrigues percolating all around us? He wasn't involved professionally, I'm convinced, but he achingly wanted to be. His seeing conspiracies behind every current event suggests that once exposed to the shadowy, secret world of spy-versus-spy it's hard to view things as being simply as they are ever again. Eventually, Ian would get a chance to participate in the swirling undercurrent of covert activity that was Beirut, but that's for a later chapter.

Chapter 25 – AL-BINAAT

Al-Binaat – Arabic for "the girls"! Ah, sweet memories. That iconic slogan of the antiwar movement – "Make love, not war!" – had no more dedicated practitioner than yours truly. With no hope of seeing Samira in the near future, I discovered that my celibatory episode in Greece with the American roommate-for-a-night had been an aberration. One look at the talent parading up and down Hamra Street had my testosterone rampaging once again. Samira, I reasoned self-indulgently, would want me to stay in practice.

There were the bevy of Western girls whose moral parameters I understood, or could just keep up with, as those parameters were constantly shifting during this epicycle in the decline of the West. What was a pleasant and unexpected surprise were the Lebanese girls. Like their Latin counterparts, they were adept at accentuating their feminine charms, sporting the shortest mini's and the lowest necklines as they strutted their stuff to appreciative male onlookers. I had to re-learn that a "come hither" look did not necessarily mean what I hoped it meant with these good Maronite and Muslim girls, no more than it did with the Catholic girls of Latin America.

On the other hand, the Beiruti girls often displayed a moral abandon antipodal to the strict conventions which constrained any sexual adventurism for village girls like Samira. Having had their traditional groundings in morality shattered by exposure to the lax mores of the much admired West, the girls of Beirut were, as the French say, *deraciné* – uprooted from their culture - and they had not acquired a new set of ground rules to regularize the mating game, other than "Do whatever you want." They were, in a word, easy.

For instance, there was the young lady I met one day while I was having lunch in a restaurant across from AUB. She was in the next booth, and, after she made eye contact that promised nice things to come, I invited her to join me at my table. Fifteen minutes later we were sharing the bed in my apartment, stark naked. Being a good Arab girl – and a Muslim one to boot – she had to preserve her virginity (We Westerners joked that the two most popular medical procedures in Beirut were nose-jobs and hymen transplants), and so sated my lust by engaging in an act a president and his intern would later make the subject of dinner table conversation.

Then there was the Iranian wife of an American graduate student in history working towards a PhD at AUB. They had sublet the living room of my apartment and the wife, Shireen, was helping me learn Arabic. The classroom was my bed, on which we would lie, side by side, grammar book propped on my belly, going over conjugations, while her husband was off studying the rise and fall of the Ottomans. The first two days of instruction it didn't occur to me that Shireen was lying closer than necessary to point out things in the text, like the derivation of the word *maktab*, "the place where things are written" from the root consonants k-t-b, "to write". The third day, as she lay there pressed up against me, one hand on my shoulder, it occurred to me. Turning towards her, I gave her a look the meaning of which could not be misinterpreted. She dropped her eyes momentarily, then raised them to mine with a look reciprocating my own. We made love, and not for the last time. (I attribute my retarded recognition of Shireen's amorous advances to the fact she was someone else's wife, my own moral roots not totally *deraciné*... yet.)

I have pleasant memories of a sweet Arab teenager who personified the deracinated promiscuity of Beiruti girls. Annette and her constant companion, Gabrielle, were high school students who hung around the AUB campus (As can be guessed from the names they were Francophile Maronite Christians). Annette was pretty;

Gabrielle was a knock-out. They favored miniskirts and disco dancing. They both had American boyfriends. They were, in sum, no village girls.

One day I was chatting with Gabrielle's boyfriend and he asked if I would mind accompanying Annette to a party that night as her boyfriend had just left for the United States. I considered Annette awfully young and virtually brain-dead, but she was pretty, so I replied, with that inimitable expression the Lebanese use to make you feel like they are doing you a big favor when in fact you have just done a whopper for them, "*Leesh la?*" – Why not?

After the party I accompanied Annette home to her parent's apartment. She invited me up for a cup of tea. The parents were out of town. We were seated in the living room and I was making my usual moves: an arm casually tossed behind her on the couch; a long, soft look into her upturned eyes; a kiss placed gently on her waiting lips. I had barely begun - not even reached down to caress her well-formed breasts - when she suggested, "Let's go into my bedroom."

"Holy shit!" I thought. I had only been hoping for some perfunctory necking.

I ended up spending the night, and a very pleasant night it was. I was floored when Annette explained her motivation for the tryst the next morning.

"I was wondering who I'd find to have sex with now that Robert's gone back to the United States", she explained.

I felt a bit used, like I was just providing stud service. But I wasn't complaining. With the fringe benefit of some very good sex, I decided Annette's company was tolerable and we became a couple. Honest as the days are long (in winter!), I told her about Samira. She assured me she didn't care, that she was just in it for the sex, but I had a feeling she wasn't being entirely truthful. In any case, the revelation of my distant true love hardly caused a ripple in the placid surface of our shallow relationship.

I tired of Annette after a month or so and tactlessly ended the romance. I call it that because I'm afraid that's what it had become for her. When I saw her reaction, I felt guilty. Not that I had lied to her about my feelings or ever held out the hope of a long-term relationship, but there was something about her innate sweetness, an innocence which belied her wanton promiscuity, which plucked at my heartstrings. It was a quality I found in Samira - in fact, in all the women who offered themselves so freely to me. I found it irresistibly appealing... and deeply disturbing.

My experiences with Arab women caused me to reflect on the concept of "the gentleman." I wondered whether gentlemen took whatever they could from women, as I did, or if they recognized a frailty in women - a yielding, guileless capability for love - which demanded protection from men's baser desires. A real gentleman, I came to conclude, offered women this protection, even from himself. He treated them... well, gently. If such men exist, and I suppose I've met a few, I respect their self-restraint, their sense of honor. I wonder if we haven't lost something important, something worth having, with the "liberation" of our women from the need for male protection, their liberation from being "ladies" to simply "women". I suspect there are more true ladies, and hence more true gentlemen, amongst the Arabs than in our own society, and our society may be the poorer for it.

Chapter 26 – VIETNAM

I thought it might be appropriate to expound more fully on my perception of our intervention in Vietnam at this point. My purpose is not to justify my course of action or sway anyone to my way of seeing things. Those of us who lived through the period have had ample time to make up our minds on the issue. A new factito here or insightful bit of analysis there isn't going to change anybody's mind at this late date. But it might be interesting for those who didn't live through those tumultuous times to hear how one confused young man of draft age, personally involved though not "in harm's way," viewed that tragic conflict in the summer of 1969.

"I have never talked or corresponded with a person knowledgeable in Indochinese affairs," wrote ex-president Eisenhower in his memoirs, "who did not agree that had elections been held as of the time of the fighting [1954], possibly 80 per cent of the population would have voted for the Communist Ho Chi Minh." To Eisenhower's way of thinking, apparently, if the Vietnamese were stupid enough to vote for a communist, it was our duty to save them from themselves. So, in the name of "defending democracy", he had his Secretary of State, John Foster Dulles, subvert an election, the one called for by the Geneva agreement of 1954 to determine the government of a united Vietnam, and prop up a compliant regime in South Vietnam which declared itself independent of the North. And the war was on, a war in which we would "wage peace" with every weapon but one in our formidable arsenal.

One can argue the justifiability of this or that policy decision, the motivations of the parties involved, the atrocities committed by one side or the other, but on the grand scale, what the Vietnam conflict was all about is not hard to fathom: it was part and parcel of the anti-colonial struggles which characterized the 20th century. Confirmation of this interpretation comes from Eisenhower himself who attributed our unwillingness to aid the French through direct military intervention as the sun set on *la mission civilisatrice* to "our tradition of anticolonialism". The poor guy lived long enough to see a new American tradition established, as we picked up right where the French left off. Let's hope the honest old warrior had turned senile before the seamier side of our actions in Vietnam became apparent.

The anti-colonial movement in Vietnam was complicated, in our eyes, by the fact it was spearheaded by communists. To Eisenhower and others in this heyday of the Cold War, America was engaged in a "never-ending struggle to stem the tide of Communist expansionism." To what extent the policy makers really believed some vast conspiracy, directed from Moscow, was manipulating events in southeast Asia or they simply used the presence of communists in the Vietnamese nationalist movement to justify actions they deemed necessary on non-ideological, strategic grounds, opinions differ. To believe the former is to insult their intelligence; to believe the latter is to label them Machiavellian.

To me, it seemed communism was first and foremost an ideology, like the beliefs (admittedly more nebulous) which reputedly undergird "the free world". I could understand its appeal to those struggling for the liberation of their nation, with its incisive Marxist-based analysis of imperialism, "the monopoly stage of capitalism", and its quasi-religious promise of a world free of exploitation. If you wanted to inspire your fellow citizens to make the sort of heroic sacrifices the Vietnamese were being asked to make, it seemed a good choice.

Regardless the ideology of his leaders, what was important was that the average Vietnamese was fighting for the same right to live securely in his own land, governed by leaders of his own choosing, that all people sought and were entitled to. Ironically, our own war of national liberation, fought for the same reasons, had inspired people around the globe, including the Vietnamese, in whose revolutionary war we now played the role of Redcoats. Tragically, we forgot our own history; in particular, the part about how a rag-tag band of committed men, emboldened by the unstinting support of their fellow citizens, could hold their own against the most powerful army in the world.

Our intervention in Vietnam was predicated on the notion that South Vietnam had been invaded by the North. The North/South terminology makes an analogy to our own Civil War tempting. By abrogating the agreement which called for the unification of North and South Vietnam in 1956, South Vietnam had, in essence, seceded. To the Northerners, there was only one, indivisible Vietnam, and the upstart Southerners were deemed as traitorous as Abraham Lincoln considered the leaders of the Confederacy. The "Yankees" in Hanoi considered it their right - their duty even - to bring the recalcitrant "Confederates" in Saigon back into "the Union".

Our intervention on the side of the South was equivalent to Great Britain, which had a strategic interest in a secure supply of cotton from the southern states for its burgeoning mills, landing troops on our shores to support the Confederacy, or would have been, had the British done so. Imagine how long drawn out and bloody our Civil War would have been had this happened! To stretch the analogy further, the British rulers could have incited their citizens' support by painting Lincoln and his gang as tools of that fomenter of atheistic libertinism (and Britain's *bete noire* at the time): revolutionary France. And just as Great Britain would have, in reality, been supporting the contemptible institution of slavery, so we were propping up a repressive social and political system in Vietnam.

Analogies are instructive only so far as they are analogous. The Civil War parallel is, admittedly, a stretch, but I think not totally devoid of usefulness. The War of Independence comparison is a better one. But if it is accurate, how did we come to act in ways so contrary to our stated aims and, if Eisenhower is to be believed, our historical tradition?

"Ve are a status quo power," Henry Kissinger, renowned geopolitical savant and unindicted war criminal, would intone in his Teutonic-accented, guttural *basso profundo*. What he meant was, "We like things the way they are." A rational - nay, brilliant - analysis of America's position in the contemporary world! But in a world where millions starve to death every year and billions live in spirit-sapping, endemic poverty, not a very Christian attitude. Definitely not a vision I was willing to risk my life or sacrifice my humanity to promote in the defoliated jungles and crater-pocked rice paddies of Vietnam.

The sad fact for Americans is that, as the world's greatest power, we have assumed the mantle of the waning imperial powers of Europe vis-à-vis the Third World. The nature of imperialism today – if I may call it that - is not as clear cut as when Indian cotton fed British mills, but the dynamics of the system remain the same: the colonies supply the raw materials, the mother country does the manufacturing; investors from the mother country supply the capital and take home the profits; the colonists do what the mother country wants or her gunboats appear off their coast. Multinational corporations, the mobility of capital, international organizations, ostensibly independent regimes, ideology-based rhetoric blur the scene, but at bottom the picture remains the same.

What it means is that for the foreseeable future, the only wars we will be fighting will be against impoverished countries trying to raise themselves out of the muck and thereby risk being seen by us as threatening our interests. A very demoralizing situation to be in for those who are called on (i.e., drafted) to defend the "status quo", especially those who are aware of what, in truth, is going on and feel any compassion for suffering humanity.

But our leaders like things the way they are. "Ve are a status quo power."

Chapter 27 – THE MEDIA

I had been impressed by the turn out of American newsmen at our march on the embassy. I didn't think they would cover any event suggesting anything but unqualified support of Israel, convinced as I was of their pro-Israel bias. I held our media responsible for the distorted understanding I had of the Arab-Israeli conflict prior to my time in Israel. It's not like I was an avid viewer of the evening news or diligent newspaper reader prior to my leaving the States. But even in my inattentive state, a false perception had been implanted in my mind. You only have to hear or read the headlines to figure out who the good guys and the bad guys are, which is about a deep as my understanding was.

I tried to remember how the media had covered the Six Day War. All I could remember was a big map of the Middle East behind Walter Cronkite showing tiny Israel surrounded on all sides by huge Arab countries - the David vs. Goliath image. That was a pretty good start on misrepresenting the situation. That most of that Arab land was barren desert, that the Arabs were hardly as one in their attitude toward Israel, that Israel was a militarist state armed to the teeth with modern weaponry supplied by its Western allies, while the Arab states most directly involved - Egypt, Syria, Jordan - were poor countries struggling to build up the toy armies left them by the departing imperialists. To explain Israel's easy victory against seemingly impossible odds, the media resorted to mythology, portraying the Israelis as supermen (an ironic take considering who else had considered themselves *Übermensch!*).

As I became an increasingly vocal proponent of the Palestinian cause, I became cognizant of the double standard applied by not only the mainstream media but the antiwar movement as well with regard to Israel. As public animosity towards what we were doing in Vietnam increased, the backflips anti-war activists and news anchors alike would perform in condemning the American war machine while praising the Zionist one became almost comical. General Westmoreland, with his sinister bushy eyebrows, was seen as a liar, an incompetent, a murderer; General Dayan, with his pirate's eye patch, as brilliant, courageous, a hero. The bombing of Cambodia in response to cross-border attacks was roundly condemned, while the bombing of Palestinian refugee camps for similar reasons was accepted as legitimate. The Geneva Convention was waved in the face of those responsible for burning Vietnamese villages, then quietly pocketed it when it came to the dynamiting of Palestinians' homes. Leftists decried apartheid in South Africa, while remaining silent on the cozy relations between Israel and the apartheid state. Most were philosophically opposed to militarism and ethnic- or religion-based states, but didn't see Israel as militaristic or comment on its ethno-religious founding principle.

Those radicals who did happened to notice these contradictions invented some shaky justifications for their hyprocrisy. Jewish radicals tried to excuse themselves on the grounds it was difficult for them, as Jews, to criticize Israel.

"Bullshit!" I thought. "If I, an umpteenth generation WASP, could be critical of my white-as-Wonder-Bread leaders, they ought to be able to criticize their fellow matzo ball-munching, dreidel-spinning Jews. Everyone else is capable of and expected to criticize their leaders when they go astray."

Gentile radicals excused the Zionists because of the Holocaust, as if that justified dumping Jewish refugees in Palestine when our own country refused to accept them. If you think Jews need their own homeland (a thought you would share with anti-

Semites, by the way), why not carve them out a piece of Germany. Wouldn't that be divine justice, no matter what god you prayed to?

The whole thing made me want to puke. As a historian, I understand the difficulty of presenting any human event in an objective way, much less such an emotion-laden, contemporary one. We all have our biases, and, strive as we may to overcome them, some are so deep-seated we're not even aware of them. But this Arab-Israeli thing was something else. It was as if no one was even trying, just as our media hadn't tried to cast a critical eye on our involvement in Southeast Asia until the mounting death toll made it unavoidable. It was the worst sort of "To the victor belongs the writing of history" distortion.

My exposure to the molders of American public opinion stationed in Beirut did little to assuage my revulsion. Foreign correspondents were as ubiquitous in Beirut as spies (some of them did double duty). Few possessed any crusading zeal, dedicated to exposing the truth no matter the cost. When taken to task by us resident Americans (who knew better the true situation than their shadows-on-the-cave-wall viewing audience back home) over some offensive article in *Time* or *Newsweek*, the correspondent responsible would blame it on his editor's marking pen. This may have been valid, but then why work for them? Not many of the journalists I met struck me as martyrs ready to sacrifice their careers to get the true story out. I doubt if any of them saw themselves as presstitutes, and I don't think they were in the sense of being willing to sell their pen to the highest bidder. I can believe they saw things the way they reported them. The genius of their employers was not in devising ways to get their correspondents to conform to the dictates of editorial policy but in selecting correspondents who saw things the way they wanted in the first place. No coercive, career-ending threats were necessary. (An unusual and instructive case was provided when Geraldo Rivera left the cozy confines of his TV show in New York City to report on location in Jerusalem. Reporting on the Israeli mop-up of the Jenin refugee camp, Rivera commented that he was a lifetime Zionist, but after seeing the conditions under which Palestinians live he was now a Palestinianist, too. No doubt he heard about that from headquarters. His response: change the subject. If he hadn't, nobody would know who Geraldo Rivera is today.)

"Class consciousness in action," I mused, disgusted.

Being young and idealistic, I lifted myself out of the puddle of my own vomit and went to work trying to remold public opinion to conform with *my* version of the truth. I worked with those Americans in Beirut organized as "Americans for Justice in the Middle East" (AJME), helping them in putting out their monthly newsletter. Eventually, I became the editor of that august publication, sent out to and widely ignored by a couple of thousand opinion-makers, news organizations, and libraries in the United States. I was proud of my contribution to the cause but never fooled myself about the futility of the effort. What impact were we likely to have in countering a media that possessed such complete and total means of thought control?

"Freedom of the press" is a wonderful thing, especially for those wealthy enough to own a printing press. In a country with a government of, by, and for the people a government-run press should, in theory, serve the people. But that's not the way we see it. Just how the mechanism for the dissemination of information evolved into its present form in our country is an interesting study. I like to look at it in theoretical terms.

Let's postulate a country where a small proportion of the population, say, five percent, possess an inordinate amount of the country's wealth and through this have gained control of the governmental apparatus. Such countries have existed and do exist, after all. Now, how would the ruling class in such a country organize a modern news media, assuming they liked their position in this hypothetical society and wished to preserve it?

One option would be to make the news media the monopoly of the government, i.e., a state-run press. Since the ruling class controls the government, they could see to it that no disturbing questions were raised which might shake the populace's inculcated belief that they lived in the best of all possible worlds. The success of this approach would vary directly with the capability of the ruling class to, well, rule well. But if some society-shaking event were to occur which shook the people out of their complacency – war, famine, plague - the control of the media by the government would cause it to be discredited to the same degree that the government was seen to be at the root of the problem.

So a really clever ruling class might adopt a more subtle approach. They'd run the news media themselves - as a class. A tax would be levied on their members to meet the cost, but this would not be a tax in the ordinary sense of the word. They would have their members buy advertisements in the media, thus funding it and assuring their class control over it. Under this arrangement, they could even allow anyone to get into the news business. Their dominance of the country's economy would assure that anyone engaging in such an enterprise would not dare offend the class interests of his advertisers if he wished to stay in business. If anyone were so foolhardy as to challenge the ruling class, he'd find himself reduced to printing his exposés on toilet paper and his readership confined to the disgruntled but perceptive few. Still, this approach entails some risk, as the malcontents, if conditions were bad enough, might be able to raise sufficient funds from the disaffected masses to interject a cacophonous squeal into the rhapsody of class-glorification. But only under conditions of societal breakdown would the ruling class not be able to drown out such discordant voices through their overwhelming economic power.

The beauty of this approach is that the press could claim independence from government control, while in fact it stifled any fundamental criticism of the ruling class. An important tactic in this misdirection would be to distract the masses with bread and circuses, i.e., celebrity gossip and human interest stories, Big Macs and the NFL. Of course, all this has nothing to do with our country, for we have no ruling class, as our right to freedom of the press proves. It's just fun to theorize. (So why do the Arabs claim our media treats us like mushrooms, saying they keep us in the dark and feed us bullshit. Must be because they don't have a free press.)

Chapter 28 – STATELESS

"He who by nature and not by mere accident is without a state," opined Aristotle, "is either above mankind, or beneath it". I wasn't without a state – I was still an American citizen - but sometimes I felt like it. Being alienated from my country made me feel alienated from all who called my country home. I was "the 'Tribeless, lawless, hearthless one,' whom Homer denounces—the outcast who is a lover of war... a bird which flies alone." He was off the mark on the "lover of war" part, but other than that Aristotle had me pegged.

So, was I above mankind or beneath it? When I view the lunacy of my fellow humans, as when they fight each other to the death, army against army, over an issue which a class of third graders could resolve peacefully, I admit to a feeling of superiority. The bogus atrocity stories, the simple-minded caricaturizing of the evil enemy, the self-righteous leaders piously professing their peaceful intent – that same class of 3rd graders could see through such tommyrot, their innate fair-mindedness not yet perverted by a tribalism inculcated through pledges of allegiance repeated zombie-like; flag-waving memorials over the fallen; phony, staged, cinematic heroism; and national anthems sung, hand on heart, on every occasion: at the start of baseball games, as a prelude to community symphony concerts (as happens in my town), even after the coming-to-order at the monthly meetings of yacht clubs (as happens at my yacht club).

The lunacy is compounded when the superficiality of the differences which turn man against man is exposed. Yesterday's enemy – vile, aggressive, blood-thirsty – is rehabilitated as today's ally – good friends, sharing our values, peace-loving. The terrorist-designated fanatics of the year before become today's heroic freedom fighters. The ever-shifting alliances driven by strategic maneuvering, which practitioners of the art liken to a game of chess, proves the lunacy. Nothing changes in the character, behavior, or methods of the players; only the geopolitics. They might as well choose up sides by flipping a coin.

"If there were no difference between men but that some were blue-eyed and some brown," I postulate - Greek philosopher like - in my more contemptuous moments. "And there was nothing to fight over but a dunghill, the blue-eyes would ban together, spread the most malicious lies about the brown-eyed, while the brown-eyes would do the same with regard to the blue-eyed; and, armed to the teeth, the two iris-differentiated factions of humanity would slaughter each other unmercifully – eyeball to eyeball - over that dunghill!"

I'm often called a contrarian by those who know me well because I will argue one side of an issue; then, when I've just about won the debate, switch sides. My disparagers think I'm just being a prick, but I see it differently. I like to think it's because I am capable of seeing both sides of an issue. Most issues have two sides – at a minimum, after all. Too many people, blinded by prejudices they are not even aware of, ignorant of facts which challenge their position, fearful of questioning beliefs that guide their lives, or corrupted by a vested interest - pecuniary or egotistic - cannot see, refuse to see, or pretend not to see the other side.

So, let me take the other side in the current debate: that I am beneath mankind. It all comes down to conceptions of brotherhood, loyalty, compassion. The State is the entity which binds one to his fellow man. It's fine to say we are "all God's chillun", but in practicality God's chillun don't all belong to the same family, except biologically speaking. The family tree has many branches and some of the branches aren't on speaking terms. In fact, they look on each other with loathing and in fear, and fear drives the members of the disparate families to huddle together for mutual security. Family ties are cemented through a common land, language, culture, history, hoped-for future. The very mechanisms which divide mankind into contending clans, tribes, nations – pledges, flags, myths, anthems – serve to unite the members of the various subspecies of the species *homo sapiens* in a near sacred, noble brotherhood.

The bonding together which unites a clan, tribe, nation provides a sense of security essential in a world wracked by internecine conflict, by unending warfare. You count on your fellow tribesmen when the tribe is threatened by the aggressive intent of another tribe, and they count on you. To prove disloyal to the tribe at such times is treasonous; not to answer the call to arms, cowardly. I agonized over these damning charges repeatedly in my eight years on the run. Perhaps the fact I could feel some guilt at least places me within the human family. It's not feeling any moral qualms over such stinging indictments which places one beneath mankind, perhaps.

Not to feel such ties to any of your fellow men (and women) smacks of a lack of compassion. If you can't feel a special affection for those closest to you – clan, tribe, nation – who can you feel compassion for? Compassion is one of those traits – like opposable thumbs and upright posture – that defines the human species. Have those incapable of showing compassion diverged from the human family tree so far as to have fallen off any branch? Was I incapable of compassion because I laughed, nay, rejoiced at the chaotic, heartrending scene atop the embassy in Saigon which marked our final departure from Vietnam? I pondered that question with much self-accusation, little self-assuredness.

"NO!" I ultimately concluded. "It's those who can feel compassion only for a portion of mankind, not mankind as a whole, who are the ones lacking in compassion. The compassion uniting bands of brothers (and sisters) too often is not extended to those outside the family, and the restriction of compassion to those you call your fellow clansmen, tribesmen, countrymen is what enables us to inflict the most unspeakable horrors on our fellow man. 'Love thy neighbor as thyself', the Good Book commands, placing such love second only to the love of God, 'Love your enemies and pray for those who persecute you.'" How many good Christians pass the test?

Clearly, the fragmented brotherliness, divisive loyalty, and truncated compassion which most of mankind seems capable of at best, always leads to conflict, to war. Sometime in the future it will lead to nuclear war, and when that happens there will be no mankind left to be above or beneath. The only rational choice, the only truly compassionate one is not to engage in that juvenile practice of choosing up sides, as if preparing for a game of tackle-the-man-with-the-ball on a school playground. If we did not succumb to, did not acquiesce in, did not let ourselves be browbeat into, did not cling in fear to a constrained notion of brotherhood, loyalty, compassion based on amorphous, artificial notions of Statehood, there could be no war.

So, I know where I stand. Let others decide whether I am above mankind or beneath it. Let others decide if I act patriotically or not. I don't aspire to be a patriot. I aspire to be a decent human being. That's the real, ultimate commitment to brotherhood, loyalty, and compassion. So I proudly stand in solidarity not with some geocentric, ethnocentric, religiocentric, ideocentric subgrouping of mankind but with all mankind. I am species-centric. I am an internationalist.

Chapter 29 – ARREST

"URGENT! FULL ADDRESS NEEDED," read the note in my mail box. I saw it was from the Dean's Office. I was suspicious. I had had two friends – a German and an American – who were active in the antiwar movement on campus, picked up by Lebanese security and unceremoniously dumped at the border with Syria a week previous (and they had been in Lebanon legally!). Despite my suspicions, I dutifully reported to the Dean's Office.

"Who needs my address?" I asked the Dean's secretary.

"Some friends," she said, I thought a bit nervously.

"Who", I asked.

"I've forgotten their names," she said, a shade paler.

"Well then, I've forgotten where I live," I spat out, turning to leave.

That evening I told my Canadian roommate, Ian, about the Dean's inquiry, and speculated it was the Lebanese *Sûreté* who wanted to know my address. Ian, always ready to see a plot behind the most insignificant of events, supported my conclusion. I had been in Beirut over two years now and had made some political contacts through my work with AJME. I gave Ian a list of people to get a hold of should I not show up at the apartment one day.

The next day, as I entered the AUB campus through the main gate, I was approached by three men, obviously *Sûreté*. They kept me preoccupied with questions as to my identity while they adroitly maneuvered me back out through the gate. Once off the campus, they informed me I was under arrest. They put me in a car and took me to a special detention center for foreigners.

I wasn't sure of the import of the arrest but remained hopeful I might be released after some questioning. The intake process at the detention center did not inspire confidence. I was led methodically and impersonally from clerk to clerk, then fingerprinted right outside a large cell full of detainees. I was tickled by the U.S. Agency for International Development emblem – the clasped hands on a red, white and blue shield – prominently displayed on the fingerprinting equipment.

"The work of some out-of-it AID official wanting the U.S. to get full credit for this contribution to the betterment of Lebanese society or the clever placement by some anti-American type who also wanted the U.S. to get full credit?" I chuckled. My chuckling stopped abruptly as the door to the cell slammed shut behind me.

"You American?" the tousled, mustachioed fellow asked as he sidled up beside where I was sitting. I didn't feel much in the mood to labor through chatting with anyone in broken English right then, but I had no choice as he went on without waiting for a response.

"My name is George," he said, extending a hand, "I am Bulgarian."

"I'm Ken," I offered, keeping it as short as possible so as not to encourage him.

"I've been in this shithole for year and half. They caught me with fake passport. I think the bastard who sold me it, he turned me in. But I am about to get out. If I find son of bitch, I kill him."

George was starting to interest me, and his English was not so bad. From his build, I judged him a man of action who very well might follow through on his threat. Hearing of George's fate, I was glad I hadn't tried that solution to my own problem. George explained that our humble abode was a way station for those either entering prison or about to be released after serving their time. Our cell mates were an assortment of Palestinian refugees, who fell under the authority of the Palestine Liberation Organization (PLO) and therefore were treated as foreigners even though they had been born in Lebanon, some Syrian laborers who had entered Lebanon illegally to find work, and one lone European, an Italian who had just completed seven months for possession of hashish.

"Each kilo, one month" he told me with a gap-toothed smile.

Having some time on our hands, George told me his life story. He and a friend had hijacked a Bulgarian airliner to Turkey after the friend killed a Bulgarian army officer in a fight. Having struck an obtuse blow for the Free World (Bulgaria was then part of the Soviet bloc), George had been hailed a "freedom fighter" and given political asylum. With travel documents from the International Red Cross, he had taken advantage of his new-found freedom of thought, speech, press, etc. to smuggle, steal, and fast-talk his way all over the eastern Mediterranean.

"It would have been all right when they caught me, but, you see, I have diamonds and stuff that did not belong to me. *Cie la vie!*" he shrugged, sliding effortlessly into another of the six languages he claimed to speak. George went on to relate some of the things he'd done before he was arrested. His adventures made mine pale by comparison. I felt like I was talking with the author of *Meetings with Remarkable Men* himself, not just a similarly gifted, unscrupulous con man.

'Your last name isn't Gurdjieff, is it, George?" I asked laughing.

"No, Yakov. Why?"

"Never mind," I said, giving him a friendly pat on the back.

"What you in for?" George asked. I told him my story.

"They deport you," George predicted. "But maybe I able to help. I know people."

Turns out, amongst all the other impressive job experiences on his resume, George had served as a bodyguard to Camille Chamoun, the Christian right-winger who had been President of Lebanon when the Marines landed in 1958. Chamoun maintained his own private army and was a formidable political force.

"Fat lot of good your contacts did you!" I thought. I wasn't sure I wanted help coming from that quarter, even if George could make good on his offer.

My jail time entered its second day without anyone telling me what I was in for or what was to happen next. Reflecting on the recent course of events I thought I figured out what had happened. I had been involved in plans for a second march, this one not organized by me but by a visiting clergyman from the States and backed by the missionary element of the foreign community. They were planning to trek down the coastal highway from Beirut to the Lebanon-Israel border on Easter weekend. I was working to add a shriller chord to the hymn-singing, pacifistic tone of the event by trying to convince the organizers to redirect the march towards the U.S. Embassy. Jack had twice warned me, in tones unusually serious for him, I'd better back off. I'd ignored the warning.

Another factor may have entered into my detention. It was Christmas time 1972 and the Paris peace talks between Secretary of State Kissinger and the Vietnamese had broken down for the umpteenth time. In response, we had commenced the carpet bombing of Hanoi and Haiphong. "World public opinion" was outraged. Some Americans were outraged, but more were shocked at the number of B-52s falling out of the sky over North Vietnam. It was a tense time for the United States government. I could believe the embassy put a request into the Lebanese government to get rid of the foreign antiwar types at AUB. Whether these factors explained why the Lebanese authorities arrested me for overstaying my non-visa or not, I still don't know.

One thing had been cleared up for me, however. I had a chance to peek at a document in the inch-thick bundle of documents in English, French, and Arabic which were passed from hand to hand during my reception ceremony at the detention center. One of them explained a mysterious episode of a year or so earlier. The letterhead displayed the name of the building in which I had shared an apartment with a fellow graduate student, a Syrian. Sulaiman, who was born in a tent on the Euphrates River - a fact reflected in his Bedouin facial tattoos - was in the habit of wearing a key chain with the emblem of the Popular Front for the Liberation of Palestine (PFLP) ostentatiously dangling out of his pocket. The PFLP was very popular amongst the students at AUB, both because it was more radical than Yasser Arafat's al-Fatah and because its leader, George Habash, and its most famous member, the pretty Leila Khaled, who had participated in the hijacking of three airliners, were both AUB grads.

I surmised the Lebanese *Sûreté* had made inquiries of our landlord about the gentleman in apartment 211 and he had panicked, envisioning a shoot-out between Palestinian factions, or a Palestinian faction and the Lebanese army, or Palestinian and Israeli commandos in the halls of his respectable establishment. On the pretense of being outraged over Annette spending the night, he kicked us out. The weird thing was he told me privately I could stay, only Sulaiman had to go. Weird because he knew Annette was *my* girlfriend. He mistakenly thought Sulaiman was the one the Lebanese *Sûreté* was inquiring about, which is comical because Sulaiman, despite his key chain, was about as political as Samira. Years later, when I had a chance to unravel the mystery for Sulaiman, then a professor at UCLA, he found it as amusing as I did.

On the third day of my detention I had a visitor. It was the Vice-Consul from the American embassy (I had so fallen into insignificance I no longer merited the Consul's attention). He repeated the Consul's offer of two years ago - that he would be happy to issue me a passport good only for direct return to the United States. The Vice-Consul was a more pleasant guy than Consul Morris. In an older-brother sort of way, he confided that many draft dodgers were getting off with suspended sentences these days. I told him I'd think about it, while mentally plotting how I might get to Australia.

Sunday morning found me mulling over the same moldy thoughts when somebody outside the cage called my name. George, guessing I might be released, ran over to me and said, "You must do favor for me. I am afraid the Lebanese send me to Bulgaria. They hang me back there. Go to Red Cross. Tell them I am here. They must protect me. It is their duty. Promise me you will do this."

I was less optimistic about being sprung, but I liked George and it didn't seem like much to ask, so I promised I would. I was escorted into the little vestibule where I had been finger-printed. While standing there waiting for something to happen, I glanced down at a newspaper lying on the guard's desk. There on the front page was my picture!

"Hey that's me!" I exclaimed. The guard quietly slipped the newspaper into the drawer of the desk. Nobody asked for my autograph.

I was taken to a much nicer, much cleaner, double occupancy cell in something called the *Hotel de Securité*. Inside was an immaculate, goateed Saudi Arabian who was munching tangerines from an enormous bag full of them while studying English. He told me he had knifed a man in a bar for insulting King Faisal. His gentle, soft-spoken manner - so characteristic of the Saudis - made it hard to believe, but I remembered reading about it in the papers.

After an hour or so in the honeymoon suite I was ushered into the office of the Director-General of the *Sûreté*, a tall, handsome military man, Colonel Antoine Daddah. The colonel had barely shaken my hand when my lawyer, Gebran Majdalani, arrived. "My lawyer" was not exactly accurate. I had met with the lawyer a couple of times as a result of my pro-Palestinian activities, but I had not hired him or even asked him to represent me. A socialist, Majdalani had enjoyed the colonel's hospitality in the past himself. It was something to watch these two political enemies outdo each other in cordiality. I imagined Majdalani fantasizing about locking the Colonel up in his own prison, while Daddah had the same dream about incarcerating Majdalani. Over Turkish coffee and some mouth-puckering confections the Arabs consider treats, the two men danced politely around the political issues of the day.

"It's appalling how little patriotism American youth have today," Daddah lamented. "I received my training at Fort Leavenworth, you know." Having established his credentials as a military expert, he went on, ""From my experience with the American military, I do not believe the United States can withdraw from Vietnam."

I thought the colonel meant the gung-ho, never-lost-a-war mentality of our pointier-headed military men would make a withdrawal under any circumstances short of victory unacceptable. I was wrong.

"I do not think the United States can withdraw from Vietnam," the colonel continued sagaciously, "because if they did, within six months the Red Chinese would be in Beirut."

I bit my tongue to give my jaw something better to do than hit the floor. Majdalani opined amiably that he didn't think the Chinese were that strong yet, then gave me a little smile, as if to say "Can you believe this idiot is in a position of power!" Later we would laugh about it, speculating on the fate of any unsuspecting Chinese who inadvertently overstayed his visa at the hands of Colonel Daddah, ever vigilant in protecting the Lebanese homeland from the reddish-yellow peril.

When he had finished his lecture on the state of the world, Colonel Daddah excused my detention as an unfortunate misunderstanding and told me I was free to go. After a round of hand-shaking and exchanging mutually insincere best wishes, Majdalani and I started for the door.

"I don't think it would be in your best interest to talk to the press," Colonel Daddah advised me as he closed the door behind us.

Chapter 30 – CELEBRITY

"There are some reporters waiting to talk to you," Mr. Majdalani informed me as we got into his car. So much had the Director-General's explicit advice made an impression on my lawyer.

"Of course Daddah doesn't want you going to the press," Majdalani sneered. "If he had his way, he'd close down half the newspapers in Beirut. Military types like him would like to see everyone marching along in lockstep, with him leading the parade. A free press hinders that. It enables the public to know in what direction he's leading us and step out of formation if it's not the direction we want to go. You know, we have a freer press here in Beirut than you do in the United States."

"He's got a point," I conceded to myself. There must be a couple of dozen newspapers in Beirut, covering the gamut of opinion – from far left to far right and everything in between. By comparison my hometown, Dallas, had two newspapers: The *Morning News* and the *Times Herald*. After the *Times Herald* folded in 1991, it only had one. There hadn't been much difference between the *Morning News* and the *Times Herald* anyway.

On the drive to his office Majdalani explained how I'd happened to get in the newspapers. My roommate, Ian, had contacted him on Saturday morning to tell him I was missing. He, in turn, had done a little asking around and found out I was in detention, so he contacted the press. This resulted in the article and photo in *An Nahar*, one of the most influential of the Lebanese papers, distributed throughout the Arab world. The Lebanese government was so embarrassed by the implication they were doing the American government's bidding in deporting me – a friend of the Arabs nonetheless! – that my old friend, Saeb Salam - still Prime Minister - had intervened to have me released.

I allowed myself to be swept along in the rush of events, not worrying about whose advice was sager, Daddah's or Majdalani's. I met with the reporters in Majdalani's office. I have to admit I was flattered having people interested in hearing my opinion on Vietnam, the Arab-Israeli conflict, the Paul Simon-Art Garfunkel breakup, etc. after years of trying to make myself heard without much success. I was interviewed by Peter Jennings, then on sabbatical from his anchorman duties to be ABC's man in Beirut. *An Nahar* wanted to do a follow-up feature on me for their Sunday supplement. My arrest and release even made *The New York Times* (it was a slow news day), under the headline "Lebanon Suspends Ouster of American Militant". I later heard Kol Israel, Israel's national radio station, reported it, too.

I thought it appropriate to write a letter to Saeb Salam thanking him for his intervention on my behalf and for the hospitality the Republic of Lebanon had extended to me through him. Through a professor I knew at AUB who was married to the prime minister's sister, I was invited to deliver the letter to the prime minister in person. He was coming to the professor's house in a few days for an informal dinner.

I showed up at the professor's house right on time. The prime minister was in the den engaged in watching himself on television, so I joined the group in the living room having drinks and chatting. They were, for the most part, prominent Palestinians, like the professor. They were discussing current events – not my trifling episode but real events – in fluent, British-accented English (I wondered if the accent was genuine or affected). These "refugees" from Palestine, most affiliated in one way or another with the American University of Beirut, I had little truck with and little sympathy for. The aristocracy of pre-Israel Palestine, I held them responsible for literally selling Palestine to the Jews and for figuratively selling out the Palestinians through their complicit, venal ties to the British mandatory power. I doubted if any of them had ever seen the inside of a refugee camp. Still, I veiled my contempt in the spirit of the occasion and enjoyed the liquor proffered by my Muslim host.

When the TV news had switched from the prime minister's doings of the day to less engaging happenings, His Excellency joined us in the living room, carnation in place and an aureole of cigar smoke ringing his countenance. I was introduced to him, or more precisely re-introduced. Mr. Salam seemed a little leery of me, as if he feared I might lash out about my incarceration or some more weighty injustice befalling mankind – like our carpet bombing of Hanoi. His restrained attitude made me wonder if there was more to the story than he was at that moment recounting; namely, how he had read of my arrest in the paper and immediately phoned Colonel Daddah to have me released.

As I was putting on my best "polite young man" impression, the prime minister gradually relaxed and adopted the jovial, expansive manner I had known from my previous encounter with him. I ventured what I meant to be a compliment: that one of my cellmates had remarked that prison conditions had improved greatly since he had come to power (George had, in fact, said this). The prime minister seemed a little unsure how to take this, either out of chagrin at receiving a compliment from a convict or because he knew that, whatever improvements may have been made, he had had nothing to do with. In any case, my *faux pas* created only a minor clitch in our amiable chat. The prime minister assured me I could stay in Lebanon as long as I liked. I could see he was anxious to reciprocate the attention being shown him by the young ladies present, so I extended a final thanks and left the illustrious gathering.

In all the hubbub surrounding my release, I didn't forget about George. Two days after my release I found out where the Red Cross office was and went by there to convey George's plea for assistance.

"Did he tell you about how he hijacked an airplane?" the Red Cross representative asked with a smirk. "He tells everyone that story. Actually, he embezzled some money from a bank with his girlfriend and they fled to Turkey. He brought enough along to buy himself political asylum, so now we have to look out for him. He's not one of our favorite charges, but we'll take care of him. He's not in any danger. They won't send him back to Bulgaria."

The Red Cross representative's story made more sense than George's self-serving one. The reputation of my cellblock hero had been tarnished; but, when I thought about it, I realized his reputation as a "freedom fighter" was little more shakily based than mine as a "war resister." In any case, within a week my reputation no longer mattered, as I was no longer of interest to anyone but myself. My fifteen minutes of fame were over. After dazzling the international press with my brilliant insights into affairs of the day, even Ian wasn't interested in my opinion on any subject more ponderous than a critique of the Lebanese wine we quaffed nightly. I settled back into the routine of a diligent graduate student. But the fallout from my brief celebrity was having one significant consequence in far-off Kuwait I was not then aware of (Did I mention Samira had moved to Kuwait a year earlier, where she was employed as a teacher?).

Chapter 31 – MARRIAGE

The Sunday after my release from jail, *An-Nahar*, the Lebanese newspaper which had first reported my arrest, carried a lengthy feature article on me, playing up the romantic side more than the political (the title was "The American Running Away… to a Palestinian"). A full-page, color photo of me graced the cover of the Sunday supplement, and inside, amongst the text, was a small, black-and-white of Samira that I had provided the paper. My picture failed to elicit so much as a single request for an autograph, but the little photo of Samira caused a sea change in my life.

Samira learned of my fate when one of her students ran up to her in the school yard in Kuwait where she was teaching waving a copy of *An-Nahar* and shouting that her picture was in the paper. For an Arab woman to have her picture in the newspaper was a *haram* (shame) no act of penance could erase. Poor Samira, she never would get a respectable Arab man - not even a cousin - to marry her now.

"Poor us", thought the brother she was living with. "We'll be stuck with her for life."

So, plucking up his courage and swearing his family to secrecy until the *fait* was *accompli*, he defied his older brother and brought Samira to Beirut to marry me. They arrived Friday afternoon. The brother had a flight back the next night as he had left a just-born son and recovering wife in Kuwait.

The first thing we did was look around for a priest to perform the ceremony. (In Lebanon, it's the religious ceremony, not the civil one, that counts.). The Greek Orthodox - Samira's denomination - refused to do it because I wasn't Orthodox (They take religious miscegenation seriously over there; they're against it). So we looked around for a cleric of my cloth. On the third try we found a protestant minister who was willing to marry us. A smooth-talking, good-looking preacher who wore designer clothes, drove a fiery red mustang, and was non-denominational except when it came to currency (he liked the big stuff). For a hundred bucks he would have married the Virgin Mary to the Devil (Samira's and my union being not quite so unholy, he only charged us fifty).

We found a little chapel and booked it for the next morning. I spread the word I was getting married amongst my friends - both of them – and the next morning half a dozen friends, acquaintances, and CIA agents - and one guy just coming in from the cold - filled the chapel to near empty as shell-shocked Samira glided down the aisle in her borrowed wedding dress to the scratchy refrain of a Handel recording. The minister was anxious to be off to the *Casino du Liban* upon completion of the ceremony, so he hurried through the marriage vows. This, along with the staccato pounding of a jackhammer being used to demolish the building next door, made it almost impossible for poor Samira, whose only familiarity with a western wedding was the staged affairs in American movies and who had not benefited from a dress rehearsal, to understand what it was she was supposed to be repeating. For the most part, she just mumbled back at the minister. He didn't seem to care and the jackhammer drowned out both hers and my responses, so the wedding came off beautifully, if of marginal legality.

The reception was held at my apartment with my co-tenant, Ian, hosting. I had wanted him to serve as Maid of Honor, Samira having none of her own. He would have done a commendable job, too, despite being straight. But the minister considered a guy maiden inappropriate, even by his loose standard of propriety. Ian's Muslim girlfriend was similarly rejected, this time because of her religion. So, an hour before the wedding I called up the wife of an American banker friend of mine, who graciously agreed to do it - despite her hardly having time to do her hair. After the ceremony, I introduced

Samira to her Maid of Honor, there having been no time to do so before then.

After seeing her brother off, Samira and I departed on our honeymoon. Jack Henderson had kindly offered the use of his chalet in the mountains, which I gratefully accepted, not wanting to look a gift horse in the mouth no matter the provenance. That night Samira proved she had saved herself for me through all those long years of separation (like she had a choice!). I didn't hang the sheet out the window Mediterranean-style, but there was the stain to prove it to my satisfaction. It caused my twisted mind some mirth to reflect that of the five boys in the family, I, the most promiscuous of the clan, was the only one to marry a virgin!

Samira moved in with Ian and me, as we were too poor to get a place of our own. It was all quite amicable, so long as Ian, a fastidious little fellow, didn't give Samira, a tidiness freak herself, too many condescending lessons in good housekeeping. Samira's and my relationship was particularly amicable: she was pregnant within two months. I continued work on my master's degree while Samira did some substitute teaching here and there. All in all, we cruised along on the sea of matrimony remarkably smoothly considering our abrupt embarkation and steerage-like quarters.

Which amazed everyone who knew our history, except Samira and me who were so naïve – or in love - we never questioned the wisdom of our union or the bizarre way in which it had come about. But what must Samira's brother have been thinking, bringing a simple "village girl" to Beirut to be married to someone she hadn't seen in three years and barely knew – and an American at that! And what must my family have thought about their prodigal brother and his exotic bride when I finally got around to breaking the news by sending them some wedding pictures? If we'd been famous enough to attract the attention of Vegas, the odds would have been 100 to 1 against the marriage lasting a year.

In the fall of 1973, after six months of marriage, I finished up work on my Master's. This had two important consequences. One was I no longer had my graduate assistanceship and the modest salary it provided. We were now living off whatever Samira could bring in through substitute teaching and an occasional job translating. The second was that my legal status in Lebanon became a bit murky. Though Saeb Salam had personally assured me I could stay in Lebanon indefinitely, I had come to understand that I had really been authorized to stay only until I completed my studies. With my studies now completed - and the possibility that Saeb Salam might be replaced any day by a less compassionate successor - I was leery of wearing out my welcome.

As a result of the publicity surrounding my arrest, I had received an offer from the Algerian ambassador to Lebanon of sanctuary in Algeria. Having waged an incredibly bloody and drawn out war of independence against the French (along the same lines the Vietnamese were now waging against us), the Algerians considered themselves in the Third World's revolutionary vanguard (though not of the communist variety). This put them in opposition to American policy on many issues. In a display of international solidarity, they had offered Eldridge Cleaver, the Black Panther ideologue, refuge from what he called political persecution (others, criminal prosecution). With my future prospects in Lebanon uncertain and feeling a need to settle down somewhere with my first child soon to be born, I decided Algeria would get to play host to a political refugee of somewhat lesser stature than Mr. Cleaver.

Chapter 32 – ALGERIA

We landed in Algeria late one night in December 1973. No one at immigration knew what to make of my *laissez-passer* signed by the Algerian ambassador, so they decided to treat us as criminals. We were taken to a police station in Algiers, Samira looking forlornly out of place with her distended belly seated on a bench wedged in between two prostitutes. My French not being up to snuff, Samira, exhausted and dazed, had to handle the communications in Arabic during our interrogation. When they finally figured out what we were all about, their attitude changed dramatically.

They took us to a compound in the hills above the city and fixed us up in one of the cottages which dotted the grounds. It was austere with its bunk beds and wood stove but comfortable enough. The next morning we learned we were being housed in what had been a summer retreat for the French during their heyday, a place called *le Centre de familial de Ben Aknoun*. It was now used to house political refugees and foreign technicians.

Some of our neighbors were Chileans who had escaped the bloody aftermath of General Pinochet's *coup d'etat*. I hoped I might find Pablo amongst them. I assumed he would have been an Allende supporter and an active one. But he wasn't there; nor could any of his compatriots tell me of his fate, as I had only a first name to identify him by. Hearing first-hand the story of what had taken place after Pinochet had come to power – the disappearance of young idealists whose bodies would later be found alongside remote country roads or floating at sea after having been pushed out of airplanes – tested my convictions. "There is no evil in the world, only ignorance", I repeated to myself mantra-like, "no evil in the world, no evil,...", but I suffered a loss of faith. The realization that my government was on the side of the murderous, privilege-defending, sanctimonious generals induced a regurgitant impulse.

The Algerians would have provided for Samira and me *gratis*; out of their commitment to international, anti-imperialist solidarity; but I didn't want to be beholden, so I found a job on my own teaching English at the University of Algiers. My legal status in Algeria was confusing to me. From discussions with Algerian officials I gathered that there was a legal distinction between political asylum and political refuge. One implied a more formal status - involving international conventions, possibly the UN - but I never understood clearly what the ramifications of each were. All I wanted from the Algerians was a place to live and work, not a handout. Eventually, through my own irresolution or cussedly independent attitude, my status in Algeria evolved into the same as it had been in Lebanon: I was allowed to stay, so long as I didn't cause any trouble because it was too much trouble for the government to do anything else about me.

I almost did not fulfill the conditions of this "contract" - through no fault of my own. A few months after arriving in Algiers I hooked up with the Reuter's correspondent in town, who convinced me to act as an unpaid stringer for him. A "stringer" is a go-fer who does the grunt work behind the stories the real reporters write. I had learned of the profession while in Beirut, where a lot of young travelers like me did this work without much in the way of credentials. For some, like Bill Blakemore of ABC, whom I knew in Beirut, it opened up a nice career. Being a foreign correspondent appealed to me and being a stringer looked like a good starting point (being unpaid, today it would be called an "internship").

One day, the correspondent, a Frenchman named Yves Legrand, had me go up to the Presidential Palace on a vaguely defined assignment to witness the return of the President from a trip abroad. I was standing outside the palace gate, notepad in hand, waiting for the presidential motorcade to arrive, when a guard came up and asked me what I was doing. I flashed my press badge, which I wore under my lapel as I had seen Yves do. The guard ushered me into the guard station beside the gate and made a telephone call. A few minutes later a black van with no markings and no windows pulled up outside, and, to my surprise, I was placed inside.

I was taken to a gloomy complex somewhere in the outskirts of Algiers, the limited view I had through the crack between the back doors of the van not enabling me to follow where we went. When we arrived and I was taken out of the van, I could see we were in front of a detention center of some sort. I was led down a corridor, past a room from which bright flashes of an electrical nature emanated, the door to the room being slightly ajar. I was locked in a cell and left there with no explanation as to who my jailers were or what offense I had committed. I correctly deduced the answer to the first question: Algerian intelligence (a no-brainer), but the answer to the second eluded me.

For two days I lay in my cell with nothing to do but read the book which had been given to me. The book, in French, was about some poor sap in Spain who had offended Franco and was being put through all sorts of tortures, mental and physical, as a consequence. Under normal circumstances I would have found the book fanciful; in the circumstances I was in, it seemed all too real, especially as my reading was sometimes interrupted by the sound of agonized screams coming from someplace down the hall.

But I didn't need the book or the screaming to convince me that my captors operated with a scary impunity. In their super-secret world and with their above-the-law authority, they could dump me in the Mediterranean and no one would even know about it, much less lodge a protest. My family back in Texas would just stop receiving the occasional letter from their remiss, wayward brother, and forever after the conversation at Thanksgiving dinners would occasionally turn to speculation as to whatever became of old Ken. And Samira, what did she think when I failed to turn up for dinner? The tears well up in my eyes, imagining her there alone in that bungalow with our newborn baby boy, so far from her own family. I personally wasn't too concerned for my safety, as I and the Algerians were on the same side, after all. This was just another one of those misunderstandings I was so good at getting myself into, which, when it was all cleared up, we'd all have a good laugh over.

The third day of my incarceration I was led into the room from which the weird, stroboscopic light had come. A personable young man in civilian clothes led my interrogation while two uniformed men stood in the background.

"How similar all these intelligence types I keep running into are," I thought, "It's as if they're cast in the same mold, just with different flags, different loyalties attached."

We communicated in French, which had to have been as taxing for my interlocutors as for me, my French being that bad. They asked me about some people in Beirut, none of whom I'd ever met or even heard of. I could tell from my questioner's increasingly friendly demeanor that he believed my answers. Either that or he was softening me up for the kill, like those Libyan sheep smugglers did those poor gazelles. When the interrogation was over, they escorted me back to my cell, still without having provided any explanation as to what my incarceration was all about.

A few hours later I was brought back to the interrogation room and asked to sign a statement. The statement was in French. As best I could make out, it stated how I had happened to be loitering outside the Presidential Palace accurately enough, but it implied some sinister machinations on Yves' part which I didn't think completely fair. I should have refused to sign it until it was translated into English, but from my own experience teaching at the university I knew it could be a while before they found someone capable of providing a translation and I hadn't seen Samira in three days. I signed it, and the black mariah took me back to the *Centre d'familial.*

Samira had taken my disappearance remarkably well, but then she took everything I inflicted upon her well. I think she was in a perpetual daze - all I subjected her to being so unfamiliar and nonsensical - and had come to accept everything I threw at her as somehow normal. It helped that she had at least known where I was after the second day, for she had been dragged in and interrogated herself, babe in arms. That must have been as trying on the interrogators as my French. I'm sure she went hysterical when, at one point, they tried to take her baby from her. In the end, they treated her decently and ~~had~~ assured her she would see her husband again. (She says the guard who escorted her into the detention facility was the spitting image – even down to his eye teeth – of the metallic-toothed villain in the James Bond movies, Jaws. Scarier than anything I experienced!)

I never did figure out why I had been detained. In a general way I would say it was because the Algerians, like others before them, just couldn't figure me out. In any case, the experience cut short my career as a foreign correspondent. It didn't do Yves' career any good, either. I heard he got kicked out of the country, probably because of that "confession" I signed. I felt bad about that. Yves was a nice guy and dedicated to his job. He and his wife had had me over for dinner. I consoled myself with the thought that maybe Yves *had* set me up to be arrested, put up to it by his contacts in the American embassy. He probably was a spy. (I get tickled how our media gets all bent out of shape when one of their own gets booted out of some country, as if a good number of them don't have second jobs!)

Chapter 33 – HABIB

Algeria was quite a different place from Lebanon. With a population of 15 million, a land area bigger than Texas, and tremendous oil and gas reserves, Algeria had aspirations of being a real country. To this end, the government imposed stringent controls over luxuries, forcing the population to save in order to have the funds to build up the country's economic base. The Lebanese recognized that their mountain domain was but a pimple on the Arab body politic. They were content for Lebanon to be a parody of a country: a hedonistic playground for the oil-rich Arabs of the Gulf, a breeding ground of shrewd traders to be sent out missionary-like to waiting markets throughout the Arab World and beyond, a juggler of the competing demands of more powerful states, surviving by compromise and craftiness, not might and main. All in all, it made for one pleasant place to living for a foreigner, and not bad for a Lebanese, either.

Both Algeria and Lebanon had been under the French, but their experiences were dramatically different. Algeria was colonized; Lebanon was ruled. Algerian society was corrupted by the intrusion of the French; Lebanese society was enriched. Algeria fought a protracted war, which cost it one-tenth of its population, to free itself from the French; Lebanon finagled its way to independence with hardly a fatality. The result was one impoverished, uneducated, defiant country and one rich, sophisticated, conciliating country.

The point of all this historical background is, of course, to compare the women in the two countries. The ultra-chic, ultra-westernized, unabashedly sensual women I had known or fantasized about knowing in Lebanon were not to be found in Algeria. There were pretty, alluringly-dressed women in Algiers, but their attractiveness was more subdued, more modest, less *pâté à la mode*, more *vin ordinaire*. The women reflected their surroundings: Beirut, all glitter and chic; Algiers: tattered French colonial.

My Algerian female students were unattainable for two reasons. First, I was married now! I might occasionally appreciate a shapely, passing female form ("married, not dead!"), but the vows of matrimony were still ringing in my ears at this point. The second reason was that the Algerian girls seemed more tied to family, more traditional than the Lebanese libertines. The French having been in their country for 130 years, in contrast to the Lebanese 30-year experience, may have given the Algerians time to adjust their mores to modern living without throwing the baby out with the bath water, i.e., becoming *deraciné*. Whatever the case, the young ladies in my classes remained unmolested by their customarily randy teacher, who didn't really miss his former passion, so all-consuming was being a husband and a father proving to be.

The void left by the abandoning of amorous pursuit of the ladies was filled by a budding relationship with a personable Tunisian named Habib (not in a sexual sense, in the sense of making life interesting). Habib was a scholar, a philosopher, and a revolutionary who broadened my horizon, providing a framework in which the contemporary situation of Algeria and countries throughout the Third World could be understood. A graduate of the University of Iowa, Habib was a colleague of mine at the *Université d'Alger*. He was living in Algeria because of some political trouble he'd gotten into in his native Tunisia. Habib was named after the man who led Tunisia to independence and ruled it for the first thirty years of the country's existence, Habib Bourguiba.

But Habib was no fan of his namesake. Habib was a Marxist. The difference between him and the President for Life of Tunisia was the difference between two magazines I discovered in Algeria and wore out my French dictionary trying to read: *Jeune Afrique*, a weekly founded by Tunisian intellectuals in 1970, and *Africasia*, another French language journal founded a year earlier. Both magazines were published in Paris and both focused their attention on the Third World - that impoverished, underdeveloped, tradition-bound, ex- or soon to be ex-colonial world in which social indicators, like the literacy rate, life expectancy, infant mortality, etc. differed so markedly from those in the two other worlds of the Cold War era (At the time the Chinese tried to present themselves as part of the Third World; they still do).

Despite occasionally being banned in the birthplace of its founders for taking too critical a line on the Bourguiba administration, *Jeune Afrique*'s editorial stance followed a moderate line on the anticolonial struggles being waged at the time, such as that of the Vietnamese. *Africasia,* on the other hand, was a firebrand, cheering on the heroic resistance of the Vietnamese.

"Nationalistic sentiments are easy to arouse in people ruled by foreigners," Habib explained as we took a break in the teachers' lounge. "This is especially true in Africa where the rulers are white and the populace black. But even in countries like mine where the outward signs are not so stark, people intuitively identify with their fellow countrymen no matter how "westernized" their compatriots may be. So the native upper class exploits this commonality to present themselves as the leaders in the anticolonial struggle. Of course, they are intimately connected through education, business, even marriage with the foreign masters they are struggling to replace." (I once watched a motorcade of Algerian big wigs pass by in Algiers. The wives were in the sedans with their husbands. All the Algerians had Western-looking wives.)

"The result," Habib went on, "is that once the nationalists have succeeded in gaining independence, they rule in the same exploitative manner as the former colonialists. It's what we Marxists call 'bourgeois nationalism'. It's a pale imitation of a truly revolutionary liberation movement. Lamentably, the new rulers are often not as competent – or honest – as the old colonial ones, so you get lopsided economic development, or no development at all, as the new oligarchs are as proficient as the old colonial regime at draining the country of its wealth. What you end up with is rampant corruption at all levels of society and constant political turmoil, leading to the overthrow of one bourgeois cabal by another, a *coup d'etat* by the military, or a real revolutionary liberation movement rising up from the oppressed masses."

"But truly revolutionary liberation movements can be bloody affairs," I pointed out. "Compare what Algeria went through to obtain its independence - an eight-year struggle in which a million Algerians were killed - with how your own country won its independence. Led by the bourgeois Bourguiba – who, incidentally, spent over 20 years in French prisons for his 'bourgeois' resistance to French rule – the Tunisian independence movement followed a gradualist approach and Tunisia gained its independence with hardly a shot fired."

"The circumstances in Algeria and Tunisia were entirely different," Habib pointed out. "France incorporated Algeria into France proper, making it a regular French *département*. A million Europeans, the *Pieds-Noirs*, settled in the country, taking over the best land. Tunisia was a French Protectorate, and there was no mass migration of foreigners into the country."

"So, was the Algerian *Front de Libération Nationale* (FLN) a truly revolutionary movement or a bourgeois nationalist movement?" I asked.

"It had to be more of a revolutionary movement because of its different circumstances. It faced much greater opposition from the mother country, so it had to win the support of the Algerian masses if it was to have any hope of succeeding. To win that support, they had to promise a revolution in the country's social/economic relations, not just a change from a French-speaking ruling class to an Arabic-speaking one."

"So, has that made for a different result in the two countries post-independence?" I asked.

"It could have, but the true revolutionaries in the FLN suffered a setback when President Ben Bella was overthrown just three years after independence by the military man still in power,

Hoari Boumediene. Boumediene undid a lot of the revolutionary acts of Ben Bella, like turning land owned by foreigners over to Algerian peasants, and adopted a more middle-of-the-road path. For instance, while supporting the Vietnamese in their fight against you Americans, he has also welcomed American investment in the country's oil industry. It was still a socialist path, but more along the lines of the European than the Soviet model. But things could change, *inshallah* (God be willing)." I shared Habib's hopes for the future and so did not point out the irony of a Marxist invoking God's help!

As the Vietnam War dragged on, I had become something of a Marxist myself. I never got very far into *Das Capital,* that weighty tome for which Marx spent years in the basement of the British library collecting minutia to prove his point. But his shorter works, such as *A Contribution to the Critique of Political Economy,* impressed me with their incisive analysis of the forces behind social dynamics. I was especially impressed with the pieces Marx wrote on our Civil War for the *New-York Daily Tribune.* Writing from far-off Paris, Marx provided, I think, a clearer understanding of the socio-economic factors – the "historical forces" - determining events in that conflict than many of our historians do even today.

Intrigued, I read further and learned things about the history of Marxism I was never taught at Dartmouth. For instance, I learned that there is no greater paean to capitalism than Marx and Engels sang in *The Communist Manifesto* of 1848:

> The bourgeoisie [i.e., capitalists], during its rule of scarce one hundred years, has created more massive and more colossal productive forces than have all preceding generations together. Subjection of Nature's forces to man, machinery, application of chemistry to industry and agriculture, steam-navigation, railways, electric telegraphs, clearing of whole continents for cultivation, canalisation of rivers, whole populations conjured out of the ground — what earlier century had even a presentiment that such productive forces slumbered in the lap of social labour?

I learned the difference between socialism (an intermediate stage on the road to a communist society, where the guiding principle is "From each according to his ability, to each according to his work") and communism (the ultimate goal, where society is organized on the principle "From each according to his ability, to each according to his need"). I read for the first time of the Second International (a confab of socialists, which resulted in a split in the movement between those who supported their country's involvement in World War I and those who did not) and the Third International (a subsequent gathering of radical socialists who opposed the war and around whose banner the various parties around the world calling themselves Communist rallied). I was surprised to learn that Britain's Labor Party subscribed to the platform of the Second International (Who knew Tony Blair is a Socialist; certainly not George Bush or his neighbors in Dallas, including my family!).

I never joined a political party (too wishy-washy for that) or subscribed to one, but I did find a philosophical foundation for my understanding of the dynamics underlying social change in Marx's dictum "It is not the consciousness of men that determines their being, but, on the contrary, their social being that determines their consciousness." To take an example at the societal level, what this means is that modern, industrialized society did not result from democratic institutions, but the other way around: the adoption of democracy resulted from the change in the "means of production" (Hegel turned upside down, as Marx described his philosophy).

Or to take an example at the personal level, it's widely held that if we just educate women they will not have so many babies. Marxists would argue, like me, that changing women's knowledge base (their "consciousness") will not cause them to modify their lifestyle (their "social being"). If you want women to have fewer babies, change their relation to the mode of production (e.g., more women in the work force), then a mentality that results in fewer babies will naturally follow. That being said, I recognize that the relationship between how we live and what we think is, sadly but assuredly, more muddled than strict Marxists or Hegelians would admit, the two history-determining factors dancing arm in arm across the stage of history in a complex, arhythmic, passionate tango that defies full understanding.

In addition to learning about Marxism, I learned something about the history of the first communist state, the Soviet Union. Instrumental in my understanding was a book called *Empire and Revolution* by David Horowitz. From Horowitz I learned things my history professors at Dartmouth somehow failed to mention; for example, that the Soviet Union had lost 20 million of its citizens (1 in 10) in World War II (we lost about 400,000, almost all military). Horowitz was a leading light of the antiwar movement in the 60s, co-editor of the leading radical periodical of the era, *Ramparts*. He later experienced an epiphany on the road to somewhere. Ironically, considering his impact on my understanding of world history, today Horowitz is an outspoken critic of the Left, i.e., many of the people I respect. Oh, if only I had seen the same light!

I often wonder what happened to my fellow "Marxist", Habib. Did he return to his native land at the head of a band of like-minded revolutionaries, intent on replacing one Habib with another as Head of State? If so, I'm afraid Habib was as out of touch with his fellow countrymen as I was to find I was with my own. Bourguiba was eventually replaced in 1987, but by a Ben Ali, not a Habib. But Habib was right about one thing: that bourgeois nationalists are not able to deliver the salvation their people need and demand. Five-term President Ben Ali was the first to go when the Arab Spring commenced 24 years later with a young Tunisian street vendor setting himself on fire.

Chapter 34 – HOMECOMING

I watched our final withdrawal from Saigon in the spring of 1975, I admit, amused. The chaotic departure of the helicopters off the embassy roof - our once figurative, now literal hangers-on desperately clinging to the skids - seemed an appropriately humiliating and comic conclusion to a war that never should have been, and never should have been so long. I felt vindicated in my refusal to participate in it, but, more charitably, I was just glad it was over. "*La guerre est finie*," I murmured to myself, totally out of context, as I watched the news on *Television Algerienne*.

The graphic symbolism of the final denouement was so clear I thought even the most dyed-in-the-wool hardliner back home must now question what we were doing in Vietnam in the first place. Most Americans may not have been lending their voices to the chorus of told-you-so's from the antiwar movement, but surely, I thought, most people saw the ludicrousness of our interventionist policy now. It was time to admit our error, mourn the dead and wounded, and attain closure, as they say these days.

I trusted that the public swing away from support for our aggressive, destructive policy would be reflected in a lenient attitude towards my own transgressions by the American judicial system. Betting my future on that assessment of the country's mood, I decided to accept the embassy's long-standing offer of a passport good only for direct travel to the United States. I would return home, after eight years on the run, so to speak, when my teaching duties at the University of Algiers ended in June.

I left Algeria with my wife and two small children on August 8, 1975. After an overnight stop in Paris, we landed at Kennedy Airport where I was met by my youngest brother, Philip. I had expected to be detained at immigration, but, despite the admitting officer's perusal of his Big Black Book of Bad Guys (and a fat book it was!), I was allowed to enter the country unmolested. I'm at a loss to explain why this was. By now thoroughly paranoid, I suspected it had something to do with the CIA, that omnipresent but never seen agency so adept at both inducing paranoia in others and succumbing to bouts of it themselves. I thought they might have had my name expunged in hopes that I might lead them to some domestic cell of Palestinian terrorists waiting to strike inside the homeland. Then again, maybe the reviewing officer just missed my name. (I know it was once inscribed therein because another brother had had a problem returning to the country from Europe a few years earlier. Many in my family wish I had acquired a *nom de guerre*.)

I prudently deposited the bomb in my suitcase (or was it a dirty diaper?) in the nearest trash receptacle instead of delivering it to my Arab co-conspirators, and, with my brother at the wheel, we all drove up to my aunt and uncle's home in Old Saybrook, Connecticut. As we headed out of New York City I was as awestruck by the affluence of America as any Third Worlder coming to the USA for the first time (and we were passing through Queens, not Manhattan!). Speeding along the Connecticut Turnpike, I ruminated on how amazed archeologists a thousand years from now will be by our incredible highway system, the way the Incas' network of roads in the Andes impress us. After eight years in the Third World, where Coca-cola is purchased not for "the drink that refreshes" but for the bottle it comes in, containers for storing olive oil and the like being that hard to come by, America appeared to me as it had to generations of immigrants: the Promised Land.

My reverie was shattered by a piece of graffiti scribbled on a highway underpass: "The American Dream is the World's Nightmare". I smiled ruefully, "How true it is." In our mindless quest to fulfill our consumptive desires, we condemn millions around the world to poverty, even starvation. To defend our right to clog our highways with gas-guzzling behemoths, to lavish a better lifestyle on our pets than many parents around the world can offer their kids, to eat ourselves into poor health with a gluttonous diet that consumes the world's harvests in a shamefully wasteful way, we bomb the wretched victims of The American Dream into submission, should they threaten our greedy lifestyle. My homecoming was already turning sour.

The sourness turned to bitter amazement as I discovered how blithely Americans ignored the lesson of the Vietnam War. The shallowness of the analysis not only by our pundits but our academicians as well of "the Vietnam experience" was appalling. Unrepentant hawks blamed the first loss in our history on the fetters placed on our brave fighting boys by "the politicians". If only they had taken the shackles off the military, we would have marched into Hanoi, maybe even Peking (What motivated the politicians to place these constraints on our generals was not addressed; it seemed to be enough just to call them "politicians".). Too many doves, even critics of the war from long before it was cool, added to the brain fog, lamenting it was "the wrong war in the wrong place at the wrong time", whatever that means. It was all a big mistake, best forgotten, was the prevailing view.

David Harris, the war resister I had known at Stanford, expressed the dismay of those of us who thought there was more to be learned from the war than this when he commented accusingly in his book, *Our War*, "A course of behavior that kills 3 million people for no good reason cannot be passed off as something for which the generic response is Excuse Me." To admit that Vietnam was not an aberration but the fruition of a policy which underlay our relations with much more of the world than just Vietnam was too heretical for anyone seeking to borrow the ear of the public to voice. Still is.

"'Those who cannot remember the past are condemned to repeat it'," I mumbled to myself, quoting Santayana to a stone-deaf crowd within earshot only of my imagination.

Hell, a lot of Americans didn't even know we'd lost the war! Or didn't care. I guess this reflected the fact that most people had not been personally involved, other than to suffer through the depressing images on the evening news every night. Some four to five million young men had experienced the fighting first-hand, but that was just 2% of the population. (Over 200,000 were charged with evading the draft. Of these, about 100,000 fled the country, most to Canada. In 1974 President Gerald Ford offered amnesty to scofflaws like me in return for two years of public service. As this implied guilt and I was not feeling at all guilty by that time, I declined the offer. In 1977 President Jimmy Carter granted a pardon to all who had dodged the draft without the public service requirement.)

The 50,000 killed? Hell, we lost more than that in one battle in the Civil War! Ironically, I may have had a closer sense of the toll the war took than most. My brothers, fortunately, had come back intact – at least physically – but the two members of my class at Dartmouth who died in the war were both fraternity brothers of mine and one of the four members of the Class of 1965 who died was a fellow Dallasite who had acted as a mentor my freshman year.

For all the reams of newsprint and miles of video footage, all the anguished hand-wringing by politicians and pundits, all the tearful looking back which would drag on *ad nauseum* over the years, the Vietnam experience hadn't made much of an impression on the American consciousness, as far as I could see. With no greater understanding of America's role in the world than we had before Vietnam, Americans seemed destined for repeat performances.

Which did not bode well for my inevitable day of reckoning with that judicial embodiment of public opinion, the courts. Neither I nor, apparently, the authorities were anxious to hasten that day. Despite Washington's instructions to the embassy in Algeria to inform them of my date and place of arrival and the embassy's quite accurate forecast in response (as I learned from files obtained subsequently), I remained at large, with no attempt on my part at concealment.

Then, one day in February 1976, six months after I had returned to the States, I responded to a knock on the front door of the family homestead in Dallas and was confronted by two gentlemen whose profession was unmistakably announced by their black-suited attire and stern, sun-glassed countenances. Having ascertained that I was one Kenneth F. Kiask, they informed me that I was under arrest for failure to comply with an order to report for induction into the armed forces of the United States of America. I let them in. They were about to cuff me when they noticed I was in my pajamas.

"Would you like to change clothes, Sir?" the younger of the two, a tough but intelligent looking fellow about my age with a humongous pistol under his arm, asked.

"Yes, I would," I replied, 'I'll just be a minute."

"I'm afraid I'll will have to accompany you, Sir," the FBI agent said.

He accompanied me up to my bedroom while his partner, a dour, older guy, guarded the front door. I had the feeling the G-men were a bit intimidated by their surroundings. The family hacienda *is* an impressive place, with a creek in front, a half-acre of prime Dallas real estate in back, and enough rooms to comfortably house us seven kids. I suspected they had not been brought up in such apparent affluence. The younger, more intelligent-looking one, looked perplexed, as if he was baffled how someone who enjoyed so many of the benefits of American society could so betray it. Or maybe he just wondered how someone with these advantages could so fuck up his life. For my part, I had to admit that, if an agency I had come to detest for its encroachment on the rights of Americans in the interest of a frightened capitalism, could win the loyalty of such a decent, intelligent young man, it couldn't be all bad.

The G-men read me my rights as they transported me downtown to the Dallas County jail. As the door clanked behind me, I reflected with sick pride that I had now been in jail on four continents (The drug-dealing folderol in Colombia; the stint in the Lebanese jail; the interrogation in Algiers; and now, my hometown hoosegow). But my hubris was tempered by the realization that, of all my incarcerations, this one was the most legitimate and the one that threatened the direst consequences.

Chapter 35 – THE TRIAL

The luck of the draw – unless you choose to believe in conspiracies – gave me Sarah T. Hughes as my judge. A woman who had achieved success in a man's world without benefit of affirmative action or anything else other than her own brilliance and tenacity, she was the judge who had sworn in LBJ while a distraught widow in a blood-stained dress looked on aboard the somber plane that carried the corpse of JFK back to Washington. She was known as the most liberal judge in the United States District Court for the Northern District of Texas, which, of course, didn't exactly make her a Trotskyite.

Assigned to represent me by the court (despite the familial trappings, I really was broke) was a crusty old, big-time lawyer very at home in Dallas. He pointedly told me at our first meeting that he wasn't particularly sympathetic towards my case. The rejoinder that if I knew his feelings on Vietnam I probably wouldn't be very sympathetic towards him either immediately came to mind, but I refrained from voicing it. One of my brothers, a lawyer also, remarked that it might not have been a coincidence that this bedrock conservative had been assigned my case. If so, I liked Judge Hughes' sense of humor in assigning him.

My lawyer assigned one of the junior members of the firm, Greg Enoch, to assist him in defending me. A personable young Texan just out of Southern Methodist Law School, Greg wore cowboy boots and carried his briefs around in a leather-bound case carved with scenes of bucking broncos and yodeling cowboys (Greg went on to become a Texas Supreme Court Justice) . He didn't know much about Selective Service law at first. I was the one who, through my own research, had determined that they couldn't prosecute me on one of the two counts I had been indicted on: failure to report for induction into the military services.

It seems that when I failed to appear for a physical as ordered, the draft board moved me up to the top of the list of those to be drafted; hence, the quick succession of the induction order after the order to report for a physical. In 1969 the Supreme Court ruled that such practices by draft boards were unconstitutional, as it represented the assumption of judicial powers to punish to which draft boards were not entitled. My order to report for induction, then, had been illegal and I could not be prosecuted for failing to obey it. All they could prosecute me on was failure to report for the physical examination, the other count of my indictment. As a basis for criminal prosecution, that sounded almost comical.

Greg was slow out of the starting gate, as they might say down at the rodeo in whatever cowtown he grew up, but he learned fast. By trial day, he was as well prepared as any young lawyer who didn't take much of a hankering to his client's case could be. I was tempted to plead guilty, as that was the honest thing to do, but my lawyers talked me out of it (They're good at that.). They argued that because I had received the notice to report for the physical after the date on which I was to report (I was in Brazil, remember.), I had not technically violated the law. The fact that I had continued to ignore the order for another seven and a half years was, in their word, moot. Sounded rather flimsy to me, but that was it. That was my defense.

The case came to trial on a Friday morning. As I entered the courtroom I saw the young FBI agent chatting with the federal prosecutor. He gave me an embarrassed nod - non-hostile; in fact, sort of sheepish. He seemed crestfallen. I speculated that he had been the one to notify the press when I was arrested, which had resulted in a reporter from the *Dallas Morning News* coming out to the house for an interview. The agent must have thought that, with all the bad press the Bureau had gotten lately, they should trumpet their success at catching a bad guy. Unforeseen by him (or me), the front-page story in the *News*, complete with a photo of me embracing my two sweet-as-molasses, beautiful babies, was quite sympathetic. In his youthful zeal for the noble pursuit in which he was engaged, I think the agent was amazed and dispirited that such a miscarriage could happen. The Bureau had come off the bad guy once again.

As Judge Hughes ordered me to rise to hear the charges against me, a momentary feeling of martyrdom came over me. I mean, here I was facing up to five years in prison, my teary-eyed wife and two innocent babes just two rows behind me. The anguish of being separated from them, to be locked up within four walls for twice as long as I had by then shared my life with Samira, would have tested my convictions had I been able to envision such a desolating outcome. Those who do not know of my inability to project myself into the future might conclude I displayed great courage standing there, risking so much in resisting those who would exploit the poor and oppress the weak. I knew it was just another case of my appearing to do something courageous, when, in fact, I had no choice but to act seemingly so because of my own stupidity, obstinacy, and just plain lack of *savoir faire*. Or so I realized once the fleeting image of martyrdom – blood dripping from the nail holes in my palms - had passed.

The trial didn't last long. I waived my right to a jury trial, figuring I stood a better chance with Judge Hughes than with twelve good men and true in a place like Dallas. Most of my fellow townsmen would have locked me up and thrown away the key without a moment's deliberation, I suspected. The prosecutor presented his case - and a good one it was, I thought. I noticed as he expounded, one of his arms was gimpy. Of about my same age, I felt a twinge of guilt, thinking his impairment might be a memento of time spent in Southeast Asia.

Greg then offered up our blarney. He was nervously going on, weakening our case the more he talked, when Judge Hughes abruptly interrupted him to rule that she found me not guilty on the grounds I had received the notice to report for the physical after the date on which I was to report. Case dismissed. After eight long, adventurous, soul-searching, life-changing years, my draft-dodging odyssey was over.

Chapter 36 – EPILOGUE

With my problems with the draft behind me, I could start to plan the rest of my life. First and foremost was the question of a career. I still favored an academic path and that led me to attend the annual convention of the American Historical Association in Washington, DC. There I learned that there were enough PhD students in history at the time that, if all the history professors in the country retired overnight, they could be replaced. With my measly M.A., the job prospects did not look too good.

But the trip was not totally in vain. I discovered that Washington was a town people actually lived in, unlike Dallas, where downtown was a ghost town after 5 PM. I had enjoyed living in cities while I was abroad, so living in a city like Washington appealed to me. I also wanted to capitalize on my years abroad by looking for a job in the field of international relations. I had taken the Foreign Service exam and passed it with ease. The next step was the interview, which was scheduled to take place in Washington in a couple of months. I wasn't so delusional as to think I would really get accepted into the State Department with my checkered past, but I had been advised repeatedly over the years by smug, pompous, boat-stabilizing careerists that if I wanted to change the system I should "work from within." I wanted to be able to say I'd tried that approach if, in the future, I tried to change the system from without. In the end, it didn't matter. As Sterling Hayden, the actor, said of himself, I was "strong enough to rebel – not strong enough to revolt". The revolution would have to go on without me.

So, a move to Washington seemed appropriate. Samira and I packed our meagre belongings into a U-Haul trailer, threw the kids in the back seat of our vintage Gremlin, and left Dallas for Washington. My dream of living in the city was shattered when we started apartment hunting. Unless we wanted to live in a black neighborhood, we couldn't afford to live in DC. I remembered the planned community of Reston from my college architectural history course, so one day we headed out into the Virginia countryside to check it out. We found it affordable and we loved the woodsy ambience, so we rented an apartment and transferred our worldly goods from the U-Haul into a two-bedroom apartment overlooking a creek. Thirty-eight years later, we're still in Reston, and still have a view of a creek.

Washington turned out to be a surprisingly small town in one respect: I kept running into people I had known in Beirut. I had already encountered my apartment mate and fellow historian, Shireen's husband, at the AHA convention two months previous. Funny encounter. He was reserved in his friendliness, as if he knew about Shireen's and my tryst, but not as openly hostile as I would have been in his place, if he did know. I didn't think too much about it, though it did occasion sweet memories of some cozy lessons in Arabic from my buxom instructor.

I ran into Brian Thompson on Pennsylvania Avenue one day. He took me up to his semi-swank office, impressive digs for one so recently removed from riding around Beirut on a beat-up motorcycle. He seemed to be well along in his career - whatever it was - while I had yet to hold a real job. I kept referring to him as a "spook" in the sort of jesting way everyone had back in Beirut, and he made it clear I'd have to drop that line if our friendship was to continue. Being utterly contemptuous of anyone who had anything to do with "The Company" by now, I kept up the jest. The friendship, if that's what it ever was, was over.

Another old friend from Beirut days I ran into in the street was Jeanne Adams. She was on her Junior Year Abroad when I knew her at AUB. She had a boyfriend back then, so there was nothing romantic between us, but I found her a fun person to be around. Now, back home, she was unattached. I was working downtown at the time, so we would get together occasionally when I was staying in town after work for some event. One night she invited me up to her apartment near Dupont Circle. As soon as we got there, she undressed (not in front of me - in her bedroom). She came out wearing a simple cloth wrapped around her, sarong-style. To remove it for amorous purposes would have required a simple flick of the wrist – mine or hers. I suspected there was nothing underneath. But whether because I still had the sacred vows of matrimony ringing in my ears or because I didn't think of Jeanne in that way (she was attractive enough, but skinny), I didn't try anything. We had a glass of wine, a nice chat, and I left her apartment as faithful to Samira as when I entered.

The interview for the Foreign Service went about as I'd expected. It didn't take long for the interviewers to discern I wasn't the sort of team player they were looking for. At the time, the foreign policy community was all atwitter over the massive amounts Saudi Arabia - flush with petrodollars from the spike in oil prices subsequent to the oil boycott of 1973 - was investing in the United States. They asked me what I thought we should do about it. I didn't show sufficient concern, pointing out that Saudi investments paled beside those of the British, the Japanese, and others.

"Besides," I blithely went on, "It's as if we're getting our oil for free. We pay the Saudis for their oil and they turn around and invest the dollars here. It's as if the dollars never left the country. What's more, their stake in the American economy gives us leverage over them. If they ever make any trouble for us, we'll confiscate their assets."

Thinking outside the box was as heralded back then as it is today, but to actually do it, was as unacceptable as it is today. Reminds me of Mark Twain's line about "those three unspeakably precious things: freedom of speech, freedom of conscience, and the prudence never to practice either." The upshot: the interviewers concluded I was hopelessly naïve in not seeing the grave threat to our national security posed by those freewheeling, *thawb*-draped Middle

Eastern sheikhs. My dream of a career in the diplomatic corps - perhaps culminating in an ambassadorship - was dashed. Would have been a nightmare anyway, maybe ending in an international incident. So the Foreign Service was out, but I did get a job in the international sphere. I was hired as a Program Coordinator at Meridian House, a government-connected outfit which provided various services to the Agency for International Development (AID).

Still interested in an academic career, I was accepted into the PhD program at the Johns Hopkins School of Advanced International Studies (SAIS). I decided against pursuing it because I feared my iconoclastic, Marxist-tinged perspective would cause me career problems down the road. I had to provide for my kids, after all. That a man with whom I would have shared a mutual disdain, Paul Wolfowitz, was later named Dean of SAIS, convinces me I made the right decision. I do know of several radical scholars I respect who have done alright in American academia, but I also know of some who have suffered professionally for their views.

When my allotted three-year tenure at Meridian House was up, I failed to obtain further employment in international affairs or anything else. After piddling around for a year or so, I landed a job on a project Computer Sciences Corporation was engaged in for the Saudi Arabian Ministry of the Interior - thanks to my wife, who worked as a translator on the project. The job was teaching technical English to Saudi trainees, who, having completed my course, would go on to learn COBOL and other computer skills. I managed to advance my expertise in computer science along with the trainees, which resulted in my getting a job as a Programmer with a consulting firm that had a contract with the Federal Highways Administration. And so began a 27-year career as a computer "scientist", mostly as a consultant to mega-corporations like MCI, Wells Fargo, and Freddie Mac. My heart was never in it, but it paid well and there was always another job when a contract ended. In 2010, upon attaining the age for full retirement benefits under Social Security, I retired.

Samira and I celebrate our 42nd wedding anniversary this year. I wish I could say the marriage has been as storybook as the romance that preceded it. It's been good, thanks to Samira and her loving, self-sacrificing ways. But after resisting the allure of Jeanne

Adams, fourteen years into the marriage I succumbed to the seven-year itch: I had an affair. It lasted six intense, nerve-wracking, pleasure-filled months. Neither of us was unhappy in our marriage or had any intention of leaving our spouse. We just felt pushed into each other's arms by a magnetic attraction we were unable to resist. That sounds like a cop out, I know, an attempt to absolve myself of responsibility for my actions, and it is. But that's how we felt. On the other hand, sometimes I wondered if we weren't just playing out the plot of a then popular movie about infidelity, *Heartburn*. Whatever the case, the guilt we felt about deceiving the ones to whom we had made a lifelong commitment cast a pall over the affair.

In the end my consort in sin confessed to her husband one night (he confessed, in turn, to having had two affairs). The extramarital interruption in an otherwise smoothly flowing marriage was over. I debated whether to tell Samira about it. Not wanting the secret to hang over our marriage, I did. I was shocked by the soul-wrenching depth of her reaction. She was disconsolate. Not being one who can give himself so unreservedly, so completely in love to another person, I had no idea how completely Samira's psychological wellbeing was grounded in our relationship. It was as if she had lost her faith in God, all the more devastating because she doesn't have a belief in that compassionate deity to console her. "She's still a simple village girl - all trust, sincerity, and innocence," I sighed ruefully, lamenting my infidelity to this day.

Despite Samira's anguish - which haunts her still - I'm glad I confessed as the episode actually strengthened our marriage. Samira started taking better care of herself and I appreciated her all the more for her devotion to me. The effect on the kids - then 13 and 12 - I still lose sleep over, fearing it shattered their precious, childhood innocence with unknowable consequences.

Looking back on those years of draft evasion, I find my history bizarre and inexplicable. Nobody who knew me back in high school or college would have predicted that this "Teenager of the Month", with a Phi Beta Kappa pin from an Ivy League school, and such a promising future would end up on the run from the law, estranged from family, friends, and country. But perhaps there is a simple explanation. In the summer between my junior and senior years at Dartmouth, I worked in New York City. One day I read in the paper that they were looking for volunteers to participate in a sensory-deprivation experiment at Columbia University. I had no idea what sensory deprivation meant, but it paid $75 and I could use the money. Turns out sensory deprivation means being deprived of your senses (Duh!). The experimenters accomplish this by having you lie on a mattress in a soundproof room, blindfolded, your arms afloat in cardboard tubes, for three days.

It never occurred to me at the time but I'm now convinced this experiment must have been part of the CIA's MKULTRA program, a mind control project utilizing drugs, hypnosis, torture, and the kind of experiment I was volunteering for (the project resulted in at least one death when an unwitting subject fed LSD jumped out a 13th-floor window). As it turned out, I was selected to be a control. I wouldn't undergo sensory deprivation; instead, I would just take a series of tests, then come back three days later and repeat the tests. I was disappointed not to be a guinea pig as being a control only paid $25; but I was probably lucky. Some of those who did take the three-day nap never fully recovered.

As part of my tests, the tester – a bored-looking graduate student – hooked up some wires attached to an electrical gizmo to my head. I asked, "You're only taking readings, right, not zapping me?" He assured me he was just taking readings. Next thing I knew I felt a slight electrical shock running through my brain. "Oops!" the aspiring Dr. Mengele apologized. I have no idea whether that little zap was intentional or a mistake, or what effect it might have had on my synapses; but if the CIA's goal in conducting the MKULTRA experiments was to turn "a typical American boy from a typical American town" (*in memoriam* Phil Ochs) into a draft-dodging, anti-imperialist internationalist, they succeeded.